# When Knowing is No Longer Enough

# WHEN KNOWING IS NO LONGER ENOUGH

TOM INGVOLDSTAD

First edition, 2026

ISBN 979-8-9949899-0-6

Independently published by Tom Ingvoldstad

www.whenknowingisnotenough.com

I want to thank my loving wife, Emi, for the unwavering support she has given me throughout this journey with no clear end in sight. This book would not exist without her.

I want to thank my late father and my mother for their support. Without them, I would not have been able to complete this endeavor.

For my children, André and Celine … you are the ones who will live this future.

…

I want to give special thanks to Heidi Arnevik for her collaboration over the years.

And finally, I want to give special thanks to the late Terje Skriver, who nudged me onto this journey thirteen years ago.

# Table of Contents

# FOREWORD

There are moments when understanding is present, yet nothing moves.

Not because insight is missing.
Not because intelligence or care is lacking.
But because something in how movement happens has quietly shifted.

Many people recognize this without having words for it.

They see what is happening.
They understand the dynamics.
They can explain the patterns with precision.

And still, the sense remains:
clarity without traction,
knowledge without passage,
awareness without movement.

This book stands inside that condition.

Not to resolve it,
but to remain with it long enough
for something else to become perceptible.

What follows is not an argument.

It does not build toward a conclusion,
nor does it ask you to adopt a position or belief.

The chapters can be entered at many points.
They do not depend on sequence in the usual way.

You may notice that meaning does not accumulate here as explanation. It gathers differently, through return, through pacing, through resonance.

What seems clear on one reading
may feel deeper, stranger, or quieter on another.

This is intentional.

This book did not arise from a desire to describe the world more accurately.

It emerged from repeated encounters with a limit …
the point where comprehension was no longer sufficient
to carry what wanted to move.

Again and again, the same realization appeared from different angles:

**The future does not emerge through understanding alone.**
**It emerges through sensing.**

This sensing cannot be instructed.
It can only be allowed.

You are not asked to read this book in a particular way.

You may read slowly or sporadically.
You may skip, pause, or return.
You may find yourself resisting certain passages
or recognizing others before you know why.

Nothing here requires agreement.

What matters is whether something registers …
not as an idea, but as a shift in attention.

The book is less concerned with what you think about what is written than with what becomes noticeable while reading.

If you reach the final pages and feel an impulse to return to
the beginning,
that movement belongs here.

The book does not progress toward an end.
It moves by deepening a field.

Each pass may reveal something slightly different …
not because the words have changed,
but because your capacity to receive has.

This foreword is not an opening statement.

It is a place you may find yourself again.

What follows does not ask you to move faster,
decide sooner,
or understand more.

It offers a space in which movement
can arise on its own terms.

Where that leads … is not guided here.

That responsibility … and that freedom …
remain with you.

…

# THE IMPASSE

## When Knowledge Stops Creating Movement

For most of modern history, progress followed a clear logic.

When information was scarce and knowledge unevenly distributed, movement depended on access. Those who could see further, understand more, or systematize what others could not, gained the ability to improve, invent, and reorganize the world.

Rational understanding was not just useful.
It was decisive.

The industrial revolution, scientific advancement, modern medicine, engineering, organizational design, and technological innovation all relied on the same underlying condition: knowledge was limited, fragmented, and costly to acquire. To understand something was already to move beyond existing patterns.

In that world, rational analysis created movement.

It allowed humans to step outside inherited structures, traditions, and constraints. It enabled improvement over repetition. It turned insight into progress.

The modern world was built this way.

Over time, this logic became so deeply embedded that we began to confuse it with reality itself. We came to believe that understanding *is* what moves systems … that clearer thinking, better models, stronger arguments, and more accurate analysis naturally led to change.

For a long time, this belief was justified.

But it is no longer accurate.
What has changed is not human intelligence.

What has changed is the condition that once gave rational understanding its power.

Information is no longer scarce.
Knowledge is no longer locked away.
Understanding how things work is no longer the primary barrier to action.

Over centuries, humanity accumulated knowledge and learned how to store, distribute, and refine it. With the Enlightenment, education, institutions, and scientific systems, access expanded steadily. What was once exclusive became increasingly shared.

Today, we are approaching the end of that trajectory.

With digital networks and artificial intelligence, humanity has entered the age of knowledge abundance. Not because every individual knows everything, but because the *system as a whole* no longer lacks access to understanding.

We can ask questions instantly.
We can explore multiple perspectives in parallel.
We can test assumptions, challenge conclusions, and retrieve accumulated insight at unprecedented speed.

The scarcity that once justified rational dominance is dissolving.

And with it, something subtle but profound is happening.

Understanding no longer guarantees movement.

Most people sense this before they can articulate it.
They know what should change … yet nothing moves.
They understand the patterns … yet repeat them.
They recognize outdated structures … yet remain inside them.

They see the flaws in systems … yet continue to operate according to the same logic.

This is not due to ignorance.
It is not due to lack of effort.
It is not due to missing information.

It is something else entirely.

The world has crossed a threshold where rational understanding alone no longer carries enough force to reorganize behavior, relationships, organizations, or systems.

We can know … and still remain stuck.

This is not a failure of rationality.
It is a signal that its historical role is changing.

Systems do not evolve because they are persuaded.

They evolve because pressure accumulates, conditions shift, and thresholds are crossed.

A system changes state when what once held it together can no longer do so. Not because the system understands this intellectually, but because continuing in the old way becomes impossible.

This is how matter changes form.
This is how ecosystems adapt.
This is how societies reorganize.
Human systems are no different.

They absorb experiences over time … successes, failures, tensions, contradictions … until a new mode of operation becomes inevitable.

From the inside, this feels like stagnation, frustration, or breakdown.

From the outside, it looks like instability or resistance.

But in reality, it is transition.

Not planned.
Not controlled.
Not argued into existence.

We now live inside such a threshold.

Knowledge continues to expand, yet movement stalls.
Insight increases, yet change lags behind.
Understanding becomes more sophisticated, yet behavior remains strangely repetitive.

This creates a paradox we will return to throughout the book:

**We have reached the end of rational dominance …**
**and knowing this changes nothing about what we do.**

This is the impasse.

And it cannot be resolved by thinking harder, explaining better, or proving more convincingly.

Because the problem is no longer what we know …
It is **what … now … creates movement.**

The end of rational dominance does not mean the end of rationality.

Analysis still matters.
Knowledge still matters.
Scientific insight remains essential.

But rational understanding is no longer the primary driver of change.

Its role is shifting … from governor to participant, from authority to interpreter, from engine to instrument.

Something else is beginning to carry movement.

…

## Knowing More Changes Nothing

We do not lack understanding.

In fact, we understand more than ever.

We understand how organizations fail.
We understand why change initiatives stall.
We understand the dynamics of burnout, resistance, power, incentives, and culture.
We understand cognitive bias, emotional triggers, systemic feedback loops, and historical context.

We can explain almost everything.

And yet … remarkably … very little moves.

This paradox does not appear first in theory.
It appears in lived experience.

People find themselves saying:

"I know this isn't working."
"I understand exactly what the issue is."
"I can see the pattern repeating."
"I know what would be healthier."
"I know what should change."

And still, nothing changes.

The same meetings repeat themselves.
The same conflicts reappear.
The same decisions are postponed.
The same structures remain intact.
The same personal habits persist.
Even when the insight is precise.
Even when the motivation is genuine.

Even when the cost of staying the same is obvious.

This creates a quiet kind of despair … not dramatic, but deeply exhausting.

Because if understanding is not enough, then what is?

For a long time, we assumed a simple sequence:

**Understand → Decide → Act → Change**

This sequence made sense when understanding itself was rare.

But something has broken in that chain.

Today, understanding often stops at itself.

Insight arrives, is acknowledged, even discussed … and then dissolves without effect.

This is why people attend workshops, read books, listen to podcasts, gain clarity …
and return to the same patterns within days or weeks.

Not because they forgot.
Not because they disagree.
But because insight no longer carries the force it once did.

The system absorbs it … and remains unchanged.

At this point, many people turn inward.

They try to understand *why* insight doesn't work.

They explore subconscious patterns.
They learn about trauma responses.

They analyze defensive behavior.
They map resistance mechanisms.

And often, this understanding is accurate.

But something unsettling happens:

Even understanding *why* we don't change
does not reliably produce change.

We can fully accept the explanation …
and still behave exactly the same way.

This is where frustration deepens.

Because now even self-awareness feels insufficient.

The paradox is often interpreted as a personal weakness.

People assume:

"I must not want it badly enough."
"I must be avoiding something."
"I must lack discipline."
"I must not be ready."

But this interpretation is misleading.

What we are encountering is not a failure of willpower or sincerity.

It is a structural limit of rational understanding itself.
Rational insight describes reality.
It does not reorganize it.

Especially not when what needs to change lives below conscious decision-making.

Most human behavior is not governed by conscious choice.

It is shaped by:
- embodied habits
- emotional memory
- subconscious protection
- social conditioning
- felt safety
- identity coherence

These layers do not respond to argument.

They respond to threat, safety, resonance, and familiarity.

Rational understanding can *see* these layers.
It can name them.
It can describe them with precision.

But it cannot command them.

This is why people can genuinely agree with an insight and still experience an immediate pull back to what is known.

Not because the insight is wrong …
but because movement is decided elsewhere.

This creates a closed loop:
- We feel tension or dissatisfaction.
- We seek understanding.
- We gain clarity.
- We attempt to apply it.
- We encounter resistance.
- We seek deeper understanding.

The loop repeats … often at a higher level of sophistication …
but without fundamental movement.

The rational mind becomes increasingly refined,
while behavior remains stubbornly familiar.

This is not regression.
It is the limit of a paradigm.

At some point, a quiet recognition emerges:

The problem is not that we don't understand enough.

The problem is that understanding is no longer the primary driver of change.

This is the paradox at the center of our time:

We have reached the end of rational dominance …
and knowing this changes nothing about what we do.

Not because the statement is false.
But because it describes a reality that cannot be altered by recognition alone.

This chapter does not offer a way out.

That is intentional.
Because the impulse to immediately resolve the paradox
is itself an expression of the old logic.

Before anything new can emerge, the system must be allowed
to fully register that its former source of movement has reached its limit.

This is uncomfortable.

It feels like standing without ground.
Like seeing clearly without being able to act.
Like knowing something is over without knowing what comes next.

But this moment is not a dead end.

It is a threshold.

And thresholds are not crossed by argument.

They are crossed when another form of movement becomes available.

…

## Systems in Motion Do Not Obey Arguments

When change fails to follow understanding, it is tempting to look for stronger explanations.

Better data.
Clearer logic.
More convincing narratives.
More compelling evidence.

But this impulse misunderstands what kind of entity we are dealing with.

Systems do not move because they are persuaded.
They move because **conditions** change.

A system evolves when the forces that hold it together no longer do so reliably.

Not because the system "realizes" something.
Not because it agrees with a new idea.
But because continuing in the old way becomes increasingly unstable.

This is true for natural systems.
It is true for biological systems.
It is true for ecological systems.
And it is true for human systems.

Change happens when accumulated pressure crosses a threshold.

Before that point, arguments bounce off the surface.
After that point, movement becomes inevitable.

Systems do not store conclusions.

They store experience.

They absorb repeated patterns of success and failure, tension and relief, coherence and contradiction. Over time, these experiences accumulate into a kind of internal memory … not conceptual, but structural.

This is why systems often continue functioning long after everyone agrees they should change.

The system has not yet accumulated *enough experience* to reorganize itself.

Understanding alone does not add pressure.
Lived contradiction does.

At a certain point, the structure reorganizes itself because the old configuration can no longer be sustained.

Organizations, institutions, cultures, and societies do not transform because someone presented a better framework.

They transform because maintaining the existing structure becomes more costly than letting it go.

Arguments appeal to the rational layer of awareness.

But systems are held together by more than rational agreement.

They are stabilized by:

- habits
- roles
- identity
- emotional safety
- power structures
- unspoken contracts
- social norms

These elements operate below conscious reasoning.

They do not dissolve because they are disproven.

They dissolve when the conditions that sustain them erode.

This is why people can agree intellectually with a critique of a system and still defend it emotionally.

The system they are part of has not yet crossed its threshold.

Modern institutions inherited a deep belief …
If we can explain something well enough, we can control it.

This belief worked when systems were simpler, slower, and more bounded.

But in complex, interconnected environments, explanation lags behind reality.

By the time a system can be fully explained, it has already changed.

This creates a widening gap between what we *understand*
and what the system is actually doing.

The more complexity increases, the less effective control through explanation becomes.

We are now inside a transition that cannot be argued into existence.

The old system is not collapsing because it has been disproven.

It is losing coherence because it can no longer hold the complexity, speed, and interdependence of the world it operates within.

This is why polarization increases.
Why resistance intensifies.
Why frustration spreads.
Why clarity coexists with paralysis.

The system is absorbing experiences faster than it can reorganize itself.

This is not failure.
It is pressure.

Resistance is often treated as something to overcome.

But in systemic transitions, resistance is information.

It signals where the old structure is still holding.
Where identity is still anchored.
Where safety is still tied to familiar patterns.

Trying to eliminate resistance through argument often strengthens it.

Because the system hears threat, not insight.

Resistance softens only when a new source of stability becomes available.

Every transition tempts us to accelerate what feels inevitable.

To push the system toward what we can already see.

But systems do not move faster because we demand it.

They move when the conditions that sustain the old configuration fall away and a new configuration becomes viable.

This cannot be forced.

It can only be **allowed**.

…

## When the Human Becomes the Limiting Factor

Once knowledge is no longer scarce, the nature of limitation changes.

For most of human history, progress was constrained by what we did not know. We lacked understanding of materials, biology, systems, and processes. Movement depended on access to information and the ability to reason about it.

Under those conditions, rational analysis was the primary driver of development. It allowed humanity to step beyond inherited patterns and create new forms of organization, technology, and society.

That era is ending.

Not because rationality has failed, but because it has succeeded.

We now live in a world where understanding how things work is rarely the main obstacle.

Information is accessible.
Knowledge is accumulated.
Analysis can be performed instantly, repeatedly, and from many perspectives at once.

Artificial intelligence did not introduce this shift.
It made it undeniable.

When rational analysis becomes abundant, it loses its position as the central constraint. The question is no longer

*"Do we understand?"*
but
*"What actually moves?"*

And this is where a new limitation appears.
As systems grow more complex, interconnected, and fast-moving, they place new demands on the humans operating within them.

Not demands for more intelligence or better reasoning, but demands for something else entirely.

The capacity to remain present inside uncertainty.
The capacity to hold tension without forcing resolution.
The capacity to sense direction without guarantees.
The capacity to act without complete justification.
The capacity to integrate conflicting signals without collapsing into reaction.

These capacities are not cognitive in the traditional sense.

They are experiential.

They live in how a human being *is*, not in what a human being *knows*.

And this is where movement increasingly slows.

It is important to be precise here.

The current impasse is often interpreted as a human deficiency: burnout, resistance, fear, avoidance, polarization, anxiety.

But these are not signs of weakness.

They are signals of mismatch.

Human systems are being asked to operate in conditions that exceed the capacities our existing structures have cultivated.

For centuries, we trained humans to optimize, analyze, plan, control, and execute. We rewarded certainty, clarity, prediction, and authority.

We did not train humans to:

stay open without knowing,
sense movement before it becomes rational,
hold contradictory truths,
or allow direction to emerge rather than be imposed.

The world now requires these capacities … but our systems do not yet recognize them as fundamental.

When knowledge was scarce, limits were external.

You could not act because the tools did not exist.
You could not change because the understanding was missing.

Now the limits appear internal.

People know what is happening.
They see the patterns.
They understand the dynamics.

And still, they feel unable to move.

This creates a deeply personal tension.

It feels like *"something is wrong with me"*
when in fact something is changing *through* us.

The pressure has not increased because humans are failing.
It has increased because the world is reorganizing around a new source of movement.

If rationality no longer governs movement on its own, something else must begin to matter.

Not instead of rationality,
but alongside it.

The emerging constraint is not intelligence, information, or knowledge.

It is the human capacity to integrate:
what is felt,
what is understood,
and what is sensed as emerging.

This capacity has always existed.
But it has never been treated as foundational.

It lived in intuition, experience, embodiment, and relational awareness … often marginalized, privatized, or dismissed as secondary.

Now, it is becoming visible because nothing else can carry the complexity of the moment.

In a knowledge-scarce world, the primary question was:
*"What should we do?"*

In a knowledge-abundant world, a different question quietly takes precedence:
*"What movement are we already in?"*

This is not a philosophical shift.
It is a practical one.

When rational analysis is always available, it no longer determines direction.
It supports it.

Movement begins elsewhere.

The bottleneck we are encountering is not a lack of answers.

It is the limit of operating from a single layer of awareness.

Systems now require humans to participate with more of themselves:
their embodied responses,
their rational clarity,
and their intuitive sensing.

Without this integration, movement fragments.
With it, coherence becomes possible again.

This is not a call for self-improvement.
It is a recognition of what the current moment demands.

This chapter does not propose a solution.

It names a condition.

The world has reached a point where the next stage of development cannot be carried by rational dominance alone.

The limitation has shifted.
The source of movement is changing.

...

## When Proof Loses Its Power

For centuries, proof has been the currency of legitimacy.

To be taken seriously, an idea had to be supported by evidence.
To move a system, a claim had to be justified.
To change direction, one had to demonstrate correctness.

This logic made sense in a world where knowledge was scarce.

When information was limited, proof protected systems from error. It slowed change, demanded rigor, and ensured that movement rested on something more stable than opinion or impulse.

Proof was not only necessary.
It was responsible.

But the conditions that gave proof its central role are changing.

Proof emerged as a way to manage limitation.

When knowledge was difficult to access, slow to verify, and costly to distribute, systems needed strong filters. Not every idea could be tested. Not every perspective could be explored. Not every claim could be validated.

Proof acted as a gatekeeper.

It determined which ideas were allowed to influence collective direction and which were dismissed. It concentrated authority in institutions, disciplines, and individuals capable of performing and judging validation.

This structure was not arbitrary.
It was adaptive.

But it was built for a world that no longer exists.

Today, the conditions have changed.

Information is no longer rare.
Verification is no longer slow.
Counterarguments are no longer inaccessible.

With artificial intelligence, vast amounts of accumulated knowledge can be accessed, compared, and explored almost instantly. Perspectives that once required years of study to encounter can now be reached in moments.

This does not eliminate the need for rigor.
But it changes where rigor lives.

When validation is abundant, centralized proof loses its role as the primary source of legitimacy.

In an age of abundance, proof no longer answers the question that matters most.

That question is no longer:
*"Is this correct?"*

It is:
*"Does this move anything?"*

A claim can be correct and still inert.
A theory can be rigorous and still irrelevant.
An argument can be sound and still fail to change behavior, direction, or structure.

This is especially true in complex systems, where outcomes are not determined by isolated facts but by interaction, perception, timing, and participation.

Proof can describe such systems.
It cannot activate them.

Proof validates statements.

Orientation guides movement.

These are not the same function.

In stable domains … mathematics, physics, engineering … validation remains essential. The cost of error is high, and the systems involved are well-defined.

But in domains like organizational development, societal change, leadership, culture, and human awareness, validation alone does not determine direction.

Here, orientation matters more than certainty.

Orientation answers questions like:

  Where is tension accumulating?
  What feels coherent?
  What is losing stability?
  What is trying to emerge?

These questions cannot be resolved by proof alone.

Proof once provided safety.

If something was proven, it could be trusted.
If it was trusted, action felt justified.
But in a world of accelerating change, proof often arrives too late.

By the time a system can be fully validated, the conditions it describes may already have shifted.

This creates a false sense of security … confidence based on what *was*, not what *is becoming*.

The result is not stability, but delay.

As proof loses its monopoly, legitimacy relocates.

Not into opinion.
Not into belief.
Not into intuition alone.

It relocates into **participation**.

Legitimacy increasingly comes from:

- lived engagement
- iterative exploration
- shared sensing
- distributed inquiry
- ongoing adjustment

This does not weaken rigor.
It distributes it.

Each individual can now explore, test, question, and validate in real time … supported by tools that make access to knowledge nearly frictionless.

The burden of proof shifts from the author to the reader.
From the institution to the participant.
From the past to the present moment.
This book does not attempt to establish authority through proof.

Not because proof is irrelevant,
but because proof is no longer scarce.

Any reader who wishes to explore, challenge, or analyze what is presented here can do so immediately … from multiple perspectives, disciplines, and traditions.

The book does not compete with that capacity.
It assumes it.

Instead of supplying justification, it offers orientation.
Instead of defending claims, it invites inquiry.
Instead of closing questions, it opens them.

In a scarcity-based system, agreement was the goal.

If enough people agreed, movement followed.

In an abundance-based system, engagement matters more than agreement.

What moves systems now is not consensus around correctness, but participation in exploration.

This is why the book does not ask the reader to believe anything.

It asks the reader to notice:
what resonates,
what resists,
what provokes,
what feels alive,
what feels inert.

These responses are not distractions from understanding.
They are data.

To stand without proof can feel unsettling.

It removes external permission.

It withdraws inherited authority.
It places responsibility closer to home.

But it also restores something that proof often replaced:
direct relationship with what is happening.

This is not the abandonment of rigor.
It is rigor relocated into lived inquiry.

The trust this book invites is not trust in its conclusions.

It is trust in the reader's capacity to engage, sense, explore, and reflect.

In an age of abundant knowledge, this is no longer idealistic.

It is necessary.

…

# Three Ways of Knowing That Were Always There

Nothing new needs to be introduced.

What follows is not a model, a framework, or a theory.
It is a description of something you already experience … even if you have never named it this way.

Long before we learned to analyze, we were already responding to the world.
Long before we could explain, we already knew how something felt.
Long before we could justify, we already sensed what mattered.

These capacities did not appear recently.
They have always been part of being human.

What is changing now is not their existence …
but their relevance.

Every experience begins somewhere other than thought.

> A tightening in the body.
> A sense of ease or unease.
> A pull toward or away from something.
> A feeling of alignment or resistance.

These responses happen before analysis.
Often before language.

They are not conclusions.
They are signals.

They tell us what feels safe, familiar, threatening, or coherent … long before we can explain why.

For most of history, these signals were treated as unreliable, subjective, or dangerous. Something to be corrected by reason.

And yet, they never stopped operating.

They simply went unacknowledged.

Soon after response comes interpretation.

We explain what we felt.
We make sense of what happened.
We compare, analyze, evaluate, and categorize.

This is the domain of rational thought.

It allows us to:
understand patterns,
test assumptions,
share meaning,
build systems,
and coordinate action.

This capacity has shaped civilization.

But it is important to notice something subtle …

Rational interpretation does not begin experience.
It responds to it.

It organizes what has already occurred at another level.

There is another way of knowing that does not fit neatly into either category.

It is the sense that something matters before you can explain why.
The feeling that a direction is right without knowing the outcome.
The recognition of potential before it takes form.

This knowing is neither reactive nor analytical.

It is directional.

It orients attention toward what wants to develop, grow, or unfold.

Many people encounter it in moments of creativity, leadership, parenting, innovation, or deep listening. Often quietly. Often fleetingly.

Because it has been difficult to validate, it has rarely been trusted.

But it has always been there.

For a long time, human systems had to prioritize one way of knowing over the others.

When survival depended on coordination, predictability, and shared understanding, rational thought became central. It offered structure and scale.

Embodied response was tolerated but controlled.
Intuitive sensing was admired but sidelined.

This separation was functional.

It allowed societies to grow beyond what intuition or embodiment alone could sustain.
But it also came at a cost.

As complexity increases, separating these ways of knowing begins to fail.

Embodied signals are still there … but ignored.
Intuitive direction is still sensed … but discounted.
Rational analysis becomes overloaded … forced to decide without access to the full picture.

This creates a familiar experience:

We know what makes sense.
We feel something else entirely.
And we struggle to reconcile the two.

Not because one is wrong …
but because they are operating without integration.

What is now emerging is not a new way of knowing.

It is the **reunification** of what was artificially separated.

Embodied response, rational interpretation, and intuitive sensing were never meant to compete.

They were meant to inform one another.

When they operate together:

the body provides signal,
the mind provides clarity,
intuition provides direction.

None dominates.
None is excluded.

Movement becomes possible again.

This integration was not feasible when rational analysis had to carry everything.

When understanding was scarce, rationality had to dominate. There was no room for ambiguity or uncertainty.

Now, with knowledge abundant and validation accessible, the system can afford something else.

It can afford to listen.
Not just to data,
but to experience.
Not just to conclusions,
but to emergence.

This is not a personal preference.
It is a structural necessity.

If you pause and reflect, you will likely recognize all three modes operating in your own life.

Moments when your body reacted before you could think.
Moments when analysis clarified what you felt.
Moments when you sensed direction without proof.

None of these were mistakes.

They were partial expressions of a whole that is now becoming visible.

The words used here are not meant to define or constrain.

They are placeholders … a way to speak about something that already exists.

You do not need to adopt this language.
You do not need to agree with it.
You do not need to remember it.

What matters is whether you recognize yourself in it.

…

## A Language for What Is Already Happening

Once something is recognized, the question changes.

It is no longer:
*"Is this true?"*

It becomes:
*"How do we speak about it without reducing it?"*

What you have encountered in the previous chapters is not a theory in need of defense. It is a pattern becoming visible … one that has been present for a long time … but lacked a shared language.

This chapter is not about defining that language precisely.
It is about making room for it.

Every major shift in how humans organize themselves requires new language.

Not because reality changes when we name it,
but because without language, what is emerging remains private, fragmented, and difficult to share.

At the same time, naming too early can freeze what is still alive.

The challenge is not to *explain* what is happening,
but to speak in a way that allows recognition without closure.

That is the role language plays here.

Much of what you have read so far may feel less like information and more like encounter.

That is intentional.

The purpose has not been to convince, instruct, or prove …
but to place you in contact with something you are already part of.

Once contact is made, participation follows naturally.

Not because you are told what to do,
but because you can no longer ignore what you notice.

In a scarcity-based world, guidance was necessary.

When knowledge was limited, direction had to be centralized.
Someone needed to know more, see further, or decide on behalf of others.

That condition no longer holds.

In a world where information, analysis, and validation are readily available, external guidance loses its organizing role.

What matters now is not instruction, but orientation.

Orientation does not tell you where to go.
It helps you notice where you already are.

From this point on, the book assumes something quietly but firmly:

You are capable of inquiry.

If something resonates, you can explore it.
If something resists, you can stay with it.
If something provokes questions, you can follow them.

You do not need the book to resolve these movements for you.

You also do not need to agree with what is written here.

Agreement is not the measure of engagement.

Attention is.

This book does not position itself as an authority on what is true.

It does not replace one framework with another.
It does not ask you to adopt a worldview.
It does not claim ownership of what is emerging.

Instead, it stands alongside you.

It offers language as a mirror … not as a mandate.

What you do with that mirror remains yours.

Section I does not conclude with answers …
It ends with a shift in stance.

You may notice that something has loosened …
    a need to be certain,
    a demand for validation,
    a pressure to decide.

Or you may notice nothing at all.

Both are fine.

What matters is that the ground has subtly changed.

…

# RESONANT CREATION

## Ideas Already Exist

Most people believe ideas begin inside us, as sparks of insight, random moments of creativity, flashes of brilliance that appear in the mind like unexpected visitors.

This is how the current system understands innovation: ideas arise in the individual, and the world waits to see if they are good enough to deserve attention, resources, and belief.

But this is not how creation actually unfolds.

When this perspective becomes visible, ideas no longer appear to originate in the mind.

**Ideas do not come from us.**
**They come to us.**

Ideas exist in what can be sensed as an Opportunity Field … a subtle, emergent layer of reality where future potentials take form long before we become consciously aware of them. These potentials live as idea-entities, each carrying an inner coherence: an understanding of the human patterns they respond to, the needs they meet, the systems they transform, and the wholeness they are oriented toward bringing into the world.

Most people have felt this phenomenon without having language for it:

- the sense that "this idea has been inside me for years"
- the feeling that an idea "arrived fully formed"
- the uncanny timing of discovering an idea the moment you were ready
- the experience of an idea that feels bigger than you

When observed closely, these are not coincidences or poetic metaphors. They are accurate descriptions of how ideas tend to operate.

Ideas exist before a founder becomes aware of them.

Founders do not invent ideas …
they enter *resonance* with ideas that want to be created.

Every idea that wants to be created vibrates across three layers simultaneously:
**Embodied subconscious patterns**
It resonates with lived tensions, longings, and embodied histories … in both the founder and the world.

**Rational understanding of reality**
It aligns with what is visible, known, and structurally ready in the market … even when this cannot yet be articulated.

**Intuitive sensing of what is emerging**
It extends beyond what exists, pointing toward a possibility the world is becoming ready to receive.

An idea becomes visible when these three layers … embodied, rational, intuitive … align in resonance.

This is why ideas often appear suddenly …
the resonance has been forming long before it is recognized.

In current systems, founders are interrogated and judged:

Are you strong enough?
Do you have the skills?
Can you execute?
Do you deserve the investment?

Creation is framed as a test of the founder.

When seen differently, this framing collapses.

The founder is not the origin of the idea …
the founder is the resonance point for its emergence.

If an idea enters a founder's awareness, it is because:

- the founder holds embodied patterns the idea responds to
- the founder possesses enough rational understanding to interpret it
- the founder has sufficient intuitive sensitivity to sense its direction

Ideas choose their founders.

Founders encounter their ideas when they are ready to receive them.

What may appear mystical from the outside reveals itself as coherent when observed through lived experience.

Ideas that want to be created carry their own inner guidance.

They "know":

- who they serve
- why they matter
- what structures need to shift
- how they bring wholeness
- what the founder will need to grow through
- what the market is ready to receive
- what the next phase of development must look like

This is why ideas often feel as if they are guiding us.

And why, when forcing gives way to listening, the next step reveals itself.

Rather than the founder proving the idea's worth, the idea demonstrates its coherence through resonance … both in the founder and in the world.

When an idea meets the market, something subtle happens.

People feel something …
even when they cannot yet explain it.

They sense a quiet recognition:

> "This makes sense, but I don't know why."
> "This feels right."
> "This solves something I couldn't articulate."
> "This is exactly what we've been waiting for."

The idea's coherence interacts with the embodied, rational, and intuitive layers of the market itself.

Markets resonate with ideas in much the same way humans do.

This is why some ideas spread naturally, even without strong marketing …
and why others struggle despite perfect execution.

It is not luck.

It is resonance.

In the current ecosystem, ideas are treated as opportunities …
something to justify, articulate, and prove.

…
Most opportunities, however, are not ideas that want to be created.

An opportunity is usually a market gap identified by rational analysis. It is built on logic, effort, and competitive positioning.

An idea that wants to be created is different:

> It carries intrinsic energy
> It has its own timing

It meets an unspoken need
It grows the founder as much as the founder grows it
It resonates before it is rationally understood
It emerges because the world is ready

Such ideas cannot be forced.

They can only be met.

When ideas that want to be created are recognized and supported, a field emerges in which they can take form.

The central question quietly shifts.

Instead of asking:
"Is the founder good enough to create this idea?"

Attention turns toward:
"What coherence is already alive in this idea … and how can the human involved grow with it?"

The idea carries direction.
The founder becomes the resonant partner.
Human potential becomes the medium through which manifestation occurs.

Recognizing the Opportunity Field changes how we see:
founders
organizations
risk
effort
human potential
the future
what is asking to be created

Ideas are not fragile sparks.

They are coherent, emergent realities … already alive …
seeking a human whose embodied patterns, rational understanding,
and intuitive sensing align enough to give them form.

…

## Tri-Level Awareness

Ideas that want to be created do not appear randomly.

They emerge through a deeper intelligence that many people sense but rarely name.

This intelligence can be described as **tri-level awareness** … the convergence of three distinct layers of human perception:

**Embodied subconscious awareness**
**Rational awareness**
**Intuitive awareness**

Each layer perceives the world differently.
Each reveals a part of reality.

But none of them … not even intuition … can reveal an idea fully on its own.

What matters is not the layers themselves, but what becomes visible when they converge.

When these three levels align, something new becomes possible …

A perspective that is:

larger than the body's reactions
deeper than the mind's interpretations
clearer than intuition's signals

This convergence gives rise to a fourth dimension of awareness … **the field of emergence**.

This is where ideas that want to be created become accessible.

To sense emergence, it helps to notice the layers that give rise to it.

**Embodied Subconscious Awareness**

*The lived interface between self and world.*

This layer is often dismissed as emotional noise, yet it holds:

ancestral patterns
ingrained reactions
deep longings
unresolved tensions
early intuitive micro-signals
unarticulated truths

This layer responds first when an idea is near.

It reacts before the mind understands anything.

The body is the earliest listener …
the doorway through which ideas begin to vibrate.

**Rational Awareness**

*The interpreter and sense-maker.*

This layer:

organizes
names
structures
analyzes
evaluates

It gives shape to the formless and coherence to the subtle.

Rational awareness is not the leader.

It functions as a bridge …
translating what emerges into forms the world can receive.

**Intuitive Awareness**
*The perceiver of what is not yet visible.*

Intuition senses:
- direction
- possibility
- future coherence
- alignment
- a sense of "rightness"

It sees the outline before the content.
It knows the destination before the path.

Yet intuition alone cannot manifest an idea.
It requires the body and the mind to ground and interpret what it perceives.

These layers are often assumed to operate separately:
the body reacts, the mind thinks, the intuition whispers.

When observed more closely, something else becomes apparent.

When embodied, rational, and intuitive awareness resonate at the same moment,
a fourth dimension emerges …

An awareness greater than the sum of its parts.

This emergent dimension feels:
- coherent
- calm
- clear
- obvious
- expansive
- deeply aligned

It is a form of intelligence unavailable to any single layer on its own.

This is the moment when ideas become visible …
not because something is "thought up,"
but because resonance with something larger becomes possible.

When the three layers triangulate, a holistic intelligence appears that:

sees beyond problems
transcends old patterns
reveals new possibilities
allows solutions unimaginable from any single level
dissolves limitations the embodied or rational layers cannot resolve

This is emergence.

It is the intelligence behind the Opportunity Field.
The intelligence behind ideas that want to be created.

Emergence is what makes an idea feel like more than a thought …
it makes it feel true,
alive,
already born.

This is also why such ideas carry emergent qualities:

they transcend the founder
they offer solutions not predictable from analysis
they carry systemic coherence
they resolve embodied tension by moving beyond it
they open new spaces rather than fixing old problems

In the prevailing system, creation is dominated by two *distorted* layers of awareness.

**Distorted embodied awareness**
Not wisdom, but emotional reactivity, suppression, stress, scarcity, avoidance, and unresolved patterns.

This layer generates pressure and urgency, but not direction.

**Overactive rational awareness**
Not clarity, but overthinking, optimization, control, linear planning, and problem-solving rooted in the past.

This layer attempts to resolve the discomfort generated by the body.

Together, these layers form a **closed loop**:

embodied tension generates pressure
the rational mind tries to fix the pressure
the fix reinforces the same underlying patterns
new problems arise from the same distortion

Meanwhile, intuitive awareness is excluded, as the system demands:

predictability
certainty
linear logic
control
proof
measurable outcomes

Without intuition, emergence remains inaccessible.

The result is familiar:

the embodied layer repeats the same emotional energy
the rational layer repeats the same conceptual solutions
nothing genuinely new appears

The system recycles itself.

Tri-level convergence releases something none of the layers can access alone:
**the field of the idea itself.**

This is why a founder may suddenly:

- see the idea
- feel its truth
- know its direction
- sense its coherence
- recognize that it has been forming long before awareness

The idea was not imagined.

It was encountered.

This leads to a simple recognition …
Ideas are emergent phenomena,
accessed through tri-level convergence,
not products of the rational mind.

Just as tri-level awareness produces a new intelligence in humans, ideas arising from emergence carry a higher coherence.

They:

- transcend personal identity
- bring clarity beyond emotional turbulence
- integrate embodied wisdom without being trapped in patterns
- exceed the limits of rational analysis
- align with future potentials sensed but not yet articulated

This is why ideas from emergence feel:

- obvious
- meaningful
- resonant
- powerful
- larger than the individual
- both new and strangely familiar

They are emergent realities …
not constructed concepts.

When the three layers align, a field of awareness becomes available that is not personal, not emotional, and not logical … but emergent.

This is where:

- ideas reveal themselves
- coherence appears
- direction becomes clear
- solutions move beyond old patterns
- creation feels guided rather than forced

Tri-level awareness is not merely a mechanism.

It is a doorway into the emergent field where ideas already exist.

…

## The Source of Emergence

Emergence does not begin with a problem.

It begins with the possibility of more.
    More experience.
    More expression.
    More life.

Not because what exists is wrong, incomplete, or broken …
but because life itself is generative.

Emergence is not corrective.
It does not arise to fix what has failed.
It arises to extend the living.

Beneath conscious thought, beneath intention and planning, there is a layer of awareness that continuously observes our lived experience.

Quiet.
Non-verbal.
Closely tied to intuition.

This layer does not judge.
It does not evaluate.
It does not intervene.

It notices …
    What we intend.
    What we do.
    What unfolds as a result.

At the same time, it senses beyond the present moment …
not as imagination or projection,
but as a subtle awareness of what could be experienced
if the system were able to move differently.

This sensing carries no urgency.
No demand.
No insistence that anything must change.

It is simply the awareness that *more* is possible.

As life unfolds … individually and collectively … experience accumulates.

Not only success and failure,
but nuance, texture, consequence, and resonance …

> Every attempt that almost worked.
> Every workaround that revealed a deeper constraint.
> Every success that felt complete …
> and every success that felt strangely hollow.

All of this is absorbed.

Not as judgment.
As information.

Over time, a quiet contrast begins to form
between what is being lived
and what could be lived.

This contrast is not dissatisfaction.

It is potential sensing itself.

Most of the time, this process remains invisible.

> Life continues.
> Systems function.
> People adapt.

Emergence does not disrupt.
It does not announce itself.
It does not demand attention.

At this stage, nothing feels unsolvable.

There is only a subtle openness …
a sense that reality could unfold further.

But experience does not stop accumulating.

As lived reality expands,
so does the sensed horizon of what could be experienced.

The gap between what is
and what could be lived
slowly grows …
    Not dramatically.
    Not urgently.
    Almost imperceptibly.

Until a threshold is approached …
    Not a rational threshold.
    Not a strategic one.

A **coherence threshold**.

The moment when the existing system can no longer quietly hold the invitation to more.

At this point, emergence shifts in nature.

What was previously sensed as possibility
now becomes a necessity … needed.

Not because something is broken,
but because something more is ready to be lived.

Emergence is no longer only forming.
It is here.

This moment *ignites* two energies at the same time.

One is the pull of what is emerging.

An independent force,
rooted in accumulated lived experience,
carrying its own coherence and direction.

It does not ask for permission.
It does not negotiate with what exists.

It simply *is*.

The other is immediate and embodied.

The reaction to what is known.
The reflex to what worked.
The protective intelligence of existing structures.

This reaction is not wrong.
It is not failure.
It is not resistance in the moral sense.

It is the system trying to preserve coherence
with the tools it already has.

The moment these two energies meet,
a distinct state appears.

What wants to be lived
and what has been lived
collide.

This state is often experienced as **the unsolvable**.

Not because no solution exists,
but because the solution does not belong
to the existing way of seeing.

For most people, what is felt first
is the embodied reaction.
    Confusion.
    Anxiety.
    Urgency.
    The sense that something is wrong.

The emergent itself remains subtle,
often unnamed,
often invisible.

For a few, the experience is different.

They sense the emergent
at the same time as they feel the resistance.

They feel the pull of what wants to be created
while standing inside the backlash of what already exists.

These are the ones we later call founders.

Not because they are special,
but because they are willing … or compelled …
to remain present in the unsolvable
long enough for something new to take form.

The unsolvable is not a flaw in the process.

It is the signature of emergence becoming real.

It marks the moment when accumulated possibility
can no longer remain latent.

From here, something must change.

Not immediately.
Not cleanly.
Not without friction.

But inevitably.

What happens next …
how systems respond,
how resistance organizes,
and how coherence is either lost or re-established …
belongs to the terrain of threshold.

…

## Founders as Points of Resonance

The contemporary narrative of entrepreneurship rests on a heavy, often invisible assumption …
that founders are the origin of their ideas.

They are expected to:

generate the idea
justify the idea
validate the idea
prove the idea
defend the idea
execute the idea
embody the idea's worthiness

This places an enormous burden on the founder …
and reflects a misunderstanding of how creation tends to unfold.

When observed differently, a different pattern becomes visible …
Founders do not originate ideas.
They resonate with ideas that arise from the emergent field.

This single shift quietly transforms the role of the founder, the nature of the idea, and the logic of creation itself.

From tri-level awareness, it becomes clearer why ideas become visible to certain people and not others.

Ideas arise from a fourth dimension of awareness … the field of emergence … which becomes accessible when embodied, rational, and intuitive awareness converge.

Founders resonate with a particular idea because:
their embodied patterns
their rational understanding
their intuitive sensitivity …
are already aligned with the emergent intelligence of that idea.

This is not coincidence.
It is coherence.

The founder is not judged.
The founder is recognized.

Recognized as someone already attuned to the idea's frequency.

This is why many founders describe the experience as:
"The idea found me."
"It arrived fully formed."
"I realize now I had been preparing for this my whole life."

These descriptions are accurate.

Ideas are emergent phenomena.

They arise from the convergence of:
embodied tensions
rational readiness
intuitive coherence
collective potentials

When an idea appears in a founder's awareness, it is because that founder has access to the same emergent field from which the idea arises.

Ideas choose founders through resonance …
not through logic, effort, or merit.

This helps explain why:

founders feel deeply connected to their idea
the idea feels larger than themselves
there is a sense of inevitability or quiet destiny
the idea is sensed long before it is understood

The founder does not invent the idea.

The founder is the first point where the idea becomes manifest.

When a founder's tri-level awareness converges with an emergent idea, the founder becomes:

the first human expression of the idea
the first container for its intelligence
the first interpreter of its form
the first embodiment of its coherence
the first place where the idea enters lived reality

This does not mean the idea belongs to the founder.

It means the founder becomes a bridge between emergence and manifestation.

This realization lifts an enormous weight:
**The founder is not responsible for creating the idea.**
**The founder is responsible for listening to it.**

The prevailing system evaluates founders through:

credentials
personality traits
performance history
leadership style
charisma
confidence
rational skill sets

These measures assess primarily the rational layer.

They overlook the embodied and intuitive layers …
and entirely miss the founder's relationship to emergence.

As a result, the system cannot reliably perceive:

resonance
alignment
coherence with the idea
capacity to grow with what is emerging

The outcome is familiar:

emergent founders are overlooked
emergent ideas are dismissed
real potential remains unseen
the ecosystem becomes blind to genuine creation

When viewed differently, another question quietly arises:

If an idea has revealed itself to a founder,
what support does that human need in order to grow with its unfolding wisdom?

This reframes evaluation entirely.

From this perspective, the founder's role becomes clearer:

**To receive**
To notice when an idea enters awareness.

**To listen**
To sense how the idea speaks through embodied, rational, and intuitive layers.

**To interpret**
To give the idea its first form, language, and coherence.

**To grow**
To expand emotionally, cognitively, and intuitively alongside the idea.

**To hold**
To become a stable container for its unfolding intelligence.

**To embody**

To allow personal development to become part of how the idea manifests.

**To release ownership**

To collaborate with the idea's wisdom rather than attempting to control it prematurely.

This is the foundation of symbiotic growth.

When a human becomes the resonance point for an emergent idea, a symbiosis begins.

The idea activates latent potential in the founder.
The founder expands to hold more of the idea's coherence.
This expansion reveals new dimensions of the idea.
Which, in turn, continues to evolve the founder.

This is why emergence feels like partnership.

And why founders often say:

"The idea is teaching me."
"I didn't know this was in me."
"I am becoming someone else through this journey."

These are not metaphors.

They describe the lived mechanics of emergent creation.

With tri-level awareness understood as the mechanism of emergence, the founder can be seen differently …

The founder does not create the idea.
The founder becomes the doorway through which the idea enters the world.

…

## When Idea and Founder Grow Each Other

When an idea that wants to be created enters a founder's awareness, something subtle but decisive happens.

Creation is no longer a one-directional act … no longer a human trying to force an idea into existence.

Instead, a symbiosis begins.

The idea begins shaping the founder,
and the founder begins giving form to the idea.

Each grows the other.

This is the core dynamic of emergent creation.

Traditional innovation models assume a linear sequence:

the founder thinks of an idea
the founder refines the idea
the founder executes the idea
the founder tests whether it works

In this view, the founder is the sole source of movement and momentum.

When observed differently, creation reveals itself as relational rather than linear.

The idea carries inherent coherence.
The founder carries inherent potential.
The relationship activates both.

This relationship begins the moment an idea becomes visible through tri-level awareness.
From that point forward, neither the founder nor the idea remains unchanged.

Ideas that want to be created do not only ask the founder to build something.

They invite the founder to become something.

Every emergent idea carries latent invitations …
specific areas where the founder will need to grow in order for the idea to take form.

An idea may invite the founder to:

- develop emotional grounding
- expand rational clarity
- trust intuitive sensing
- grow beyond inherited patterns
- release the need for control
- open to collective creation
- step into forms of leadership long avoided

These invitations are not demands.

They are activations.

The founder grows because the idea creates conditions where growth becomes both necessary and natural.

The idea reveals the next stage of the founder's evolution.

This is why founders often say:

> "This idea is asking more of me than I expected."
> "I need to grow to keep up with it."
> "I can feel it pulling me into a new version of myself."

This is not pressure.

It is emergence.

The founder's growth is part of the idea's intelligence.

Just as the idea activates the founder, the founder gives the idea its first form in the world.

This form is not arbitrary.

It reflects:

- embodied resonance
- rational understanding
- intuitive sensitivity
- the founder's current stage of growth

In this sense, the founder becomes the first living prototype of the idea.

The idea expresses itself through the founder's awareness, skills, relationships, language, and worldview.

This is why:

- similar ideas take different forms through different founders
- two humans sensing the same emergence may activate different potentials
- no emergent path can be replicated
- no two ideas manifest in the same way

The founder's uniqueness becomes part of the idea's identity.

The idea grows through the founder …
and the founder becomes the vessel through which the idea enters the world.
Symbiosis does not begin and end when an idea "arrives."

It continues through every stage of creation:

**Emergence**
The idea activates awareness.
The founder recognizes it.
**Early forming**
The idea offers direction.
The founder experiments with shape.
**Expansion**
The founder grows to meet what the idea invites next.
The idea expands as the founder expands.
**Alignment**
Behaviors, skills, and patterns adjust.
The idea clarifies its scope and path.
**Manifestation**
The idea becomes real.
The founder becomes capable of delivering it.

This movement is not linear.

It is cyclical … like breathing.

Each phase influences the next.
Each evolves alongside the other.

This is the living engine of emergent creation.

When symbiosis is overlooked, several familiar breakdowns appear.

Ideas stall when founders do not grow …
not because the founder is inadequate,
but because the idea's next phase required a new level of embodied, rational, or intuitive capacity.

Founders struggle when they disconnect from the idea …
not because the idea loses value,
but because inner coherence drifts from the emergent intelligence.

Ideas accelerate when founder and idea grow together …
which is why emergent creations often move quickly once resonance is aligned.

From this perspective, risk also looks different.

The risk is not primarily in the idea.
It is in the ability to remain in symbiosis.

A detail often missed:

Ideas evolve because the founder evolves.

As the founder:

releases old patterns
expands intuitive sensitivity
gains rational clarity
deepens embodied wisdom

the idea:

reveals more of itself
increases in complexity
gains coherence
clarifies its unfolding direction
becomes more potent

Ideas do not arrive fully formed.

They unfold through the founder's growth.

This is why founders say:

"The idea is changing shape."
"I see something now that I didn't see before."
"It's becoming clearer each day."

This is not drift.

It is emergence responding to evolution.

Conventional approaches ask founders to generate strategy from:

- fear
- speculation
- market mapping
- competitive analysis
- predicted trends
- intellectual logic

When symbiosis is recognized, this burden eases.

Direction emerges from the relationship itself.

The idea signals its next movement.
The founder senses it.
The founder grows into it.
The idea expands as the founder matures.
The next step becomes apparent.

No forcing.
No guessing.
No pushing.
No "shoulds."

The idea is not a puzzle to solve.

It is a path that reveals itself.
When symbiotic growth is recognized, creation ceases to be:

- a personal struggle
- a burdensome responsibility
- a lonely endeavor
- a test of worthiness

It becomes:

a partnership
a co-creation
a shared unfolding
a living dynamic between human and idea
a journey of becoming

…

## From Unicorn Hunting to Idea Harvesting

Every innovation system rests on a theory of risk.

The contemporary startup ecosystem … accelerators, venture capital, incubators, angel networks, corporate innovation … is shaped by a single assumption:

**Ideas are uncertain, unpredictable, and inherently risky.**
Therefore, the system must place many bets to find a few winners.

This assumption quietly shapes everything:

investment strategies
founder evaluation
accelerator design
portfolio theory
funding terms
power dynamics
the language of "pivots," "runways," and "fail fast"
the mythology of unicorns

When observed more closely, this assumption begins to fracture.

Not because it is immoral or misguided …
but because it does not align with how ideas actually emerge or how creation unfolds.

A different pattern becomes visible …

The risk is not in the idea.
The risk lies in the system's ability to grow with what is emerging.

This single shift changes how everything else is perceived.

The prevailing system struggles to recognize ideas that want to be created because it operates through a narrowed perception …

**embodied pressure and emotional avoidance**
**rational optimization and market reasoning**

with intuitive awareness largely excluded.

Without intuition, there is no access to emergence.
Without embodied wisdom, subconscious dynamics remain unseen.
Without convergence, the idea's inherent coherence cannot be perceived.

This limitation forces the system to:

**Treat all ideas as equally uncertain**
Because it cannot sense which ideas already contain coherence.
**Spread bets across many startups**
Because resonance and alignment cannot be detected early.
**Expect high failure rates**
Because emergence is neither recognized nor supported.
**Overvalue extreme outcomes**
Because overwhelming scale must compensate for structural blindness.
**Attribute risk to the idea itself**
Because the actual source of risk … lack of growth and resonance … remains invisible.

A self-reinforcing loop forms:

ideas are treated as risky
bets are spread widely
most fail
failure confirms the assumption
control increases
distortion deepens

The system produces its own evidence
and mistakes repetition for truth.

When ideas are seen differently, risk appears differently.

Ideas that want to be created are not unstable.
 They are coherent.
 They are emergent.
 They carry their own intelligence.

The idea becomes the stable point.

Attention shifts to a different question:

Can the founder, the team, and the surrounding ecosystem grow with the idea's unfolding evolution?

This is where risk actually lives.

Not as uncertainty …
but as a threshold of growth.

Every emergent idea invites specific growth from those involved:
- emotional
- rational
- intuitive
- relational
- structural
- existential

This is the symbiotic growth described earlier.

When ideas falter in conventional systems, it is rarely because:
- the idea lacked merit
- the market was not ready
- the timing was wrong
- the product was imperfect
- the founder lacked experience
- the strategy was flawed

These are outcomes, not causes.

The underlying cause is simpler:

The human system could not grow at the pace the idea required.

This is the growth gap.

Conventional systems rarely perceive this gap.
They assess ideas through metrics and founders through performance.

When growth is observed directly, different signals become visible:

- resonance
- embodied alignment
- intuitive coherence
- emergent potential
- growth invitations
- subconscious resistance
- relational fractures
- energetic mismatch

This allows risk to be sensed long before outcomes appear.

When emergence cannot be perceived, innovation becomes a form of gambling.

When emergence is recognized, a different posture becomes possible.

Rather than betting on ideas, attention turns toward cultivating those already alive.

This reframes risk:
**Success becomes more probable**
Coherence and resonance make development more predictable.

**Failure rates diminish**
Because failure reflects unsupported growth, not random chance.
**Capital becomes developmental**
Supporting people and systems, not spreading speculative bets.
**Portfolio logic loosens**
Fewer ideas are needed when coherence is present.
**ROI expectations normalize**
Risk resembles traditional business risk rather than extreme volatility.
**Ecosystems calm**
Evaluation gives way to support; extraction to participation.
**Access broadens**
Resonance and growth are human capacities, not exclusive traits.

This is not idealism.

It is a different way of seeing.

**Idea-centric risk** asks:
Does the idea make sense?
Does the market want it?
Is the technology proven?
Is the founder good enough?
Will it scale?

Its assumption:
**The idea is risky.**

**Growth-centric risk** asks:
What growth does this idea invite?
Where might subconscious patterns distort the journey?
What emotional and intuitive support is needed?
What structures must form, and when?
Can the ecosystem hold this coherently?

Its assumption:
**The idea is coherent.**
**Risk lies in the system's capacity to grow.**

Innovation shifts from speculation to cultivation …
from gambling to gardening.

In conventional systems, success is rare because:
- most ideas are not emergent
- founders are misaligned
- intuition is suppressed
- growth is unsupported
- resistance is unmanaged
- structure forms too early
- ecosystems fragment
- pressure distorts coherence

When emergence is centered, a different pattern appears:
- Ideas begin with coherence
- Founders are already aligned
- Growth is supported directly
- Resistance is part of the process
- Structure forms at the right moment
- Intuition leads unfolding
- Ecosystems participate rather than judge

Success becomes a result of alignment,
not statistical luck.

When risk is seen this way, consequences ripple outward:

funding models shift
accelerator design evolves
founder evaluation softens
portfolio logic loses dominance
capital flows change
support structures mature
risk becomes manageable
innovation re-centers on human process

The focus moves
from hunting unicorns
to harvesting emergence.

…

# Human Potential as Foundation

In every era of human history, a shift occurs in what the world recognizes as its most valuable resource.

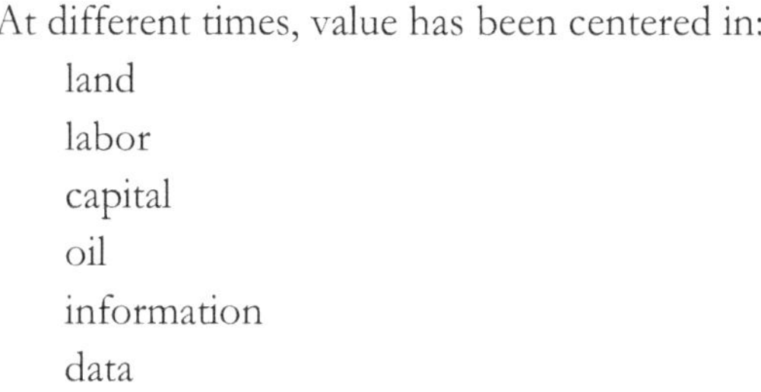

At different times, value has been centered in:

land
labor
capital
oil
information
data

Each shift has reshaped society, economics, and power structures.

We are now entering another shift … one the prevailing system has difficulty fully perceiving:

Human potential is becoming the most valuable resource on the planet.

Not human labor.
Not effort.
Not productivity.
Not compliance.
Not optimization.

Human potential … the integrated capacity of the embodied, rational, and intuitive dimensions of a human being … is emerging as a primary driver of creation, innovation, and collective evolution.

This chapter explores why this is becoming visible now.

Conventional systems have largely been built on extraction:
extracting labor
extracting value
extracting efficiency
extracting performance
extracting compliance
extracting productivity

The consequences are familiar:
burnout
disconnection
emotional suppression
intuitive dulling
rational rigidity
systemic stagnation

Many people sense that something essential is missing in how we work and organize … even if they cannot yet name it.

What becomes visible is this:

**Human beings have been treated as components in a machine, rather than as sources of emergent intelligence.**

Systems built this way struggle to access emergence,
because human potential is neither recognized nor supported.

Human potential is often confused with:
talent
intelligence
creativity
personality
motivation

These are expressions, not the source.

Human potential arises from the integration of three dimensions:

**Embodied awareness**:

Emotional coherence, grounded presence, felt truth, subconscious alignment.

**Rational awareness**:

Knowledge, articulation, discernment, framing, structural clarity.

**Intuitive awareness**:

Emergent sensing, directionality, future coherence, perception beyond the visible.

When these dimensions integrate, a fourth quality becomes apparent:

This is the same emergent field described earlier …
now expressed not only through ideas, but through the human being themselves.

Human potential is this emergent intelligence.

It appears as:

adaptive
fluid
creative
deeply aware
relational
intuitive
systemically coherent
self-correcting
purpose-oriented
inherently regenerative

This is precisely what emergent ideas resonate with.

Which is why human potential becomes the foundation of creation.
Human potential is not new.

What is new is that it is becoming necessary.

The structures that once held society together were designed for:

stability
predictability
control

They strain under conditions of:

complexity
rapid change
systemic interdependence
cultural fragmentation
technological acceleration
existential uncertainty

The world has become more complex than linear intelligence can manage.

What begins to matter now is emergent intelligence …
the intelligence that arises through integrated human awareness.

This is why:

intuition gains importance
emotional literacy becomes a leadership capacity
embodied trauma work enters the mainstream
creativity shifts from novelty to coherence
relational fields matter more than individual performance
rigidity collapses under pressure
flexible, resonant systems endure

This shift is not being created.
It is being recognized.

Human potential is not merely personal.

It is the precondition for ideas that want to be created.

Ideas arise from the emergent field,
and only humans with integrated awareness can perceive them.

A mutual relationship becomes visible …

Ideas need human potential to take form.
Human potential grows through engagement with ideas.

Through this relationship, humans are able to:
- hear what is emerging
- feel its coherence
- understand its meaning
- interpret its direction
- give it form
- grow alongside it

Ideas, in turn, invite humans to:
- release outdated patterns
- expand intuitive sensitivity
- develop new rational structures
- embody deeper emotional coherence
- open to collective creation
- step into new versions of themselves

This is the symbiotic relationship underlying emergence.

Earlier we saw that:
the idea is not the risk
the risk lies in the growth gap
systems must grow with what is emerging

Human potential becomes the foundation of this inversion.

As human potential activates:
- resonance strengthens
- coherence stabilizes

emergence becomes accessible
reactivity softens
clarity increases
alignment deepens
relational fields mature
resistance loosens
direction clarifies

A simple pattern emerges:
**High human potential corresponds with a higher probability of success.**
**Low human potential manifests as instability, friction, and distortion.**

Many failures previously attributed to ideas
are better understood as failures to support human potential.

When human potential becomes central, creation changes character.

It is no longer industrial.

It becomes developmental.

To create something new:
founders grow
teams grow
ecosystems grow
relationships reorganize
new capacities emerge

Creation becomes a path of becoming.

Human potential is not a consumable resource.

It is a regenerative engine.

Systems built around it tend to produce more potential than they use … in contrast to extractive systems, which consume more than they replenish.

Human potential does not stop at the individual.

When integrated awareness becomes common, collective structures shift:

new ways of working appear
leadership reorganizes
organizations reconfigure
decision-making evolves
economic logics change
political systems soften

Groups begin to operate from collective emergence:

decisions improve
coherence increases
conflict diminishes
alignment deepens
intelligence expands
adaptation accelerates
trust grows

What becomes visible is the outline of a different kind of society … one organized around resonance, potential, and emergence rather than control.

Human potential is not a soft idea.
It is a structural foundation.

It helps explain:

- why ideas emerge
- why founders resonate
- why symbiosis works
- why risk inverts
- why success stabilizes
- why old models fracture
- why new systems form

Human potential is the ground of creation.

It is the intelligence through which the future becomes possible.

…

## Distributed Resonant Ecosystems

In the earlier chapters, we explored:

how ideas emerge
how founders resonate
how symbiosis unfolds
how risk inverts
how human potential becomes central

Taken together, these observations point toward a simple realization:

Creation is not individual.
Creation is collective.
Creation is relational.
Creation is distributed.

This is not a philosophical claim.
It is a structural pattern.

No emergent idea comes into the world through a single person.
No founder can manifest what is emerging alone.
No system transforms through isolated effort.

Emergent creation requires ecosystems …
and ecosystems require an operating logic aligned with emergence rather than hierarchy.

What becomes visible is a different kind of collective organization: **distributed resonant ecosystems**.

Many organizational and societal structures rest on assumptions that once worked well:

**Authority sits at the top**: Decisions flow downward.
**Information must be controlled**: Knowledge is centralized and protected.
**People are resources**: Value is measured by output, efficiency, and compliance.

These assumptions functioned in stable, predictable environments.

They strain under conditions of:
- rapid change
- complexity
- interdependence
- emergent ideas
- intuitive leadership
- distributed intelligence
- co-creation

Hierarchical systems were shaped for a world that no longer exists.

They are not failing because they are wrong …
but because they are incompatible with emergence.

Distributed resonant ecosystems arise when:
- multiple people
- multiple roles
- multiple capacities
- multiple forms of awareness

begin operating as a coherent field rather than as fragments.

Their logic differs fundamentally from control-based systems.

In resonant ecosystems:
- sensing is shared
- intuition circulates
- embodied awareness moves through the group
- insight arises from many points
- decisions emerge rather than descend

Leadership shifts.

The "leader" is no longer the one who commands,
but the one who attunes the field.

Decision-making becomes field-based rather than hierarchical … making the system more adaptive and responsive.

In control-based systems, order is maintained through force.

In resonant ecosystems, coherence renders force unnecessary.

Coherence arises from:
- shared resonance with what is emerging
- aligned human potential
- clarity of direction
- relational integrity
- embodied trust
- intuitive attunement

When coherence is present, effort collapses.
When coherence is absent, control cannot compensate.

This is why resonant ecosystems often feel:
- alive
- fluid
- safe
- directed
- intelligent

They do not rely on pressure.
They rely on alignment.

In rigid systems:
- roles are fixed
- job descriptions are static
- hierarchy defines contribution
- people fit into predefined boxes

In resonant ecosystems:
roles shift as the idea evolves
contribution follows resonance
responsibility moves to where energy is alive
people step forward when called
growth reshapes capacity

A role is not a box.
It is a point of resonance.

This fluidity allows systems to adapt without crisis, reorganization, or bureaucracy.

Growth in resonant ecosystems is not individual.

It is collective.

As what is emerging unfolds:
founders grow
co-founders grow
early contributors grow
advisors grow
partners grow
the ecosystem itself grows

Growth distributes across the system
rather than concentrating on a single figure.

This dissolves:
pressure
burnout
isolation
ego-identification
internal competition

And replaces them with:
- mutual expansion
- shared resonance
- relational coherence
- collective purpose

Resonant ecosystems begin to resemble organisms rather than machines.

Traditional organizations:
define structure first
then attempt to fit people and ideas into it

Resonant ecosystems:
- sense emergence first
- allow structure to crystallize organically
- adapt structure as what is emerging evolves

Structure becomes:
- flexible
- responsive
- intelligent
- intuitive
- alive

This mirrors how living systems organize.

A resonant ecosystem is more than a group of aligned people.
It is a shared field of awareness.

Within this field:
- intuitive signals move freely
- embodied information circulates
- insight arises coherently
- decisions self-organize
- emotional safety stabilizes

conflict resolves through awareness
direction becomes clear

Without the field, there is a team.
With the field, there is an ecosystem.

When human potential is active
and ecosystems are resonant,
risk diminishes further.

Distributed awareness makes the system:
adaptive
responsive
coherent
stable
intelligent
emotionally grounded
intuitively aligned

Such ecosystems can:
recognize opportunity early
adjust direction organically
catch blind spots
stabilize tension
distribute load
absorb shocks
maintain coherence
Movement becomes smoother …
not because effort increases,
but because resistance decreases.

In hierarchical systems, leadership often means dominance.

In resonant ecosystems, leadership becomes attunement.

Attunement involves:

- listening
- sensing
- perceiving
- holding
- grounding
- clarifying
- stabilizing

Leaders become:

- focal points
- resonance anchors
- coherence holders
- field stewards
- containers for emergence

This is not a softer form of leadership.

It is a more comprehensive one …
working with the full spectrum of human and collective intelligence.

Distributed resonant ecosystems are not limited to organizations.

They point toward new collective arrangements:

- economic systems grounded in growth rather than extraction
- governance rooted in coherence rather than control
- communities organized around relational intelligence
- education shaped by human potential
- political systems guided by emergent decision-making

What is emerging is not an abstract vision.

It is already taking form wherever resonance replaces domination.

…

# HUMAN POTENTIAL

## Work as a Space for Human Flourishing

Work is not a neutral part of human life.

It is one of the primary environments in which human beings develop:

emotionally
relationally
cognitively
intuitively
psychologically
existentially

It is where people learn who they are.
Where they meet their patterns.
Where they encounter their limits.
Where they sense their longings.
Where they discover their potential.

For centuries, work has been organized around extraction, efficiency, and control.

That logic is no longer viable … economically, psychologically, or systemically.

A shift is becoming visible, emerging from people's lived experience:

Work is moving
from a space of extraction
toward a space of human flourishing.

This chapter explores why this shift is no longer optional …
and how a different way of working is already beginning to take form.

The prevailing model of work rests on three assumptions:

Humans are resources

Productivity is the primary measure of value
Control is the primary mechanism of coordination

The symptoms of this model are familiar:
burnout
disengagement
stress and anxiety
emotional suppression
diminished creativity
fragmentation
distrust
political conflict
superficial collaboration
misalignment between values and actions

Most people recognize these symptoms intimately,
even if they lack language for what is missing.

The world is changing faster than extractive systems can adapt.

Models built on control cannot sustain:
complexity
rapid adaptation
emergent ideas
intuitive sensing
relational dynamics
distributed intelligence

Their breakdown is not a failure.

It is an invitation.

Across cultures and generations, a quiet shift is underway.
People are withdrawing from work systems that treat them as:
replaceable
limited

predictable
controllable
purely rational
disconnected from meaning

This withdrawal takes many forms:
emotional disengagement
the search for purpose
boundary-setting
leaving corporate roles
choosing independent paths
burnout-driven exits
intuitive career shifts
longing for authenticity
dissatisfaction with hierarchy

This is not laziness.
Not entitlement.
Not weakness.

It is human potential pressing against environments too small to hold it.

People are beginning to sense:
what they are capable of
what they want to contribute
the deeper truth within them
the mismatch between their potential and their surroundings

Human potential is rising.
Old systems are reaching their limits.

When seen differently, work is not separate from human development.

Work *is* development.

It becomes:

a mirror for subconscious patterns
a field for embodied awareness
a place to refine rational clarity
a training ground for intuitive intelligence
a space for relational coherence
a container for emotional growth
a practice of self-integration
a place to meet emergence

In resonant creation, ideas invite the founder to grow.

In resonant work environments, the same dynamic appears collectively:

**The work grows the person,**
**and the person grows the work.**

This is the essence of flourishing.

Flourishing is not comfort.
It is growth.

It is the expansion of one's capacity to:

sense
feel
understand
integrate
create
align
act

Work becomes a place where human beings evolve into their next selves.

Flourishing is no longer optional.

It has become a structural requirement.

**Emergent ideas require emergent people:**
Innovation cannot arise through suppression. It requires coherent, open nervous systems.

**Distributed ecosystems require relational maturity:**
Trust, attunement, and relational intelligence become essential.

**Complexity requires intuitive sensing:**
No rational model alone can keep pace.

**Creativity requires emotional coherence:**
Suppression constricts vision; coherence opens it.

**Adaptation requires embodiment:**
Emergence cannot be met from the neck up.

**Meaning sustains engagement:**
People commit deeply only to work that resonates.

**Human energy becomes the primary currency**
Not time.
Not effort.
Not presence.

Aligned, coherent, intuitive human energy
becomes the foundation of value creation.

In this context, flourishing shifts
from "nice to have"
to central operating condition.

When work is organized around resonance and coherence, its character changes.

Work begins to:
align with emergent direction
feel lighter as coherence replaces force
become relational rather than transactional
invite personal evolution

be guided by sensing rather than control
activate growth through challenge
honor humanity as intelligence rather than obstacle

This does not make work soft.

It makes work potent.

Because flourishing is the condition
that allows emergence to move through people and systems.

As work becomes a space for flourishing, extraction naturally recedes.

There is less need to:
push
manage
control
incentivize compliance
suppress intuition
deny emotion

And more room for:
alignment
resonance
shared vision
mutual growth
clarity
emergent insight
relational coherence
Work shifts from struggle
to possibility.

Organizations soften from machines
into living ecosystems.

Teams evolve from roles
into distributed intelligence.

A quieter truth begins to surface …

Work can become a space of healing.

Not because it turns into therapy …
but because it aligns with human potential.

When work resonates:
    subconscious patterns integrate
    emotional tension releases
    relational wounds soften
    leadership becomes authentic
    clarity replaces confusion
    potential activates
    identity expands

Work becomes a container
where people discover who they are becoming.

This is not utopian.

It is emergent.

It is already happening …
this language simply makes it visible.

Work is being redefined.
    Not by policy.
    Not by strategy.
    Not by tools.
    Not by industrial logic.

But by:

emergence
resonance
coherence
human potential
collective intelligence
distributed ecosystems

Work becomes one of the most powerful environments for human development and societal transformation.

…

## Organizations as Living Ecosystems

To sense what organizations are becoming, it helps to release what they have been.

The organizations most people know were built on a powerful metaphor:

**An organization is a machine.**

This metaphor quietly shaped everything:

roles as components
leadership as control
people as resources
strategy as engineering
culture as lubrication
processes as machinery
KPIs as measures of output
hierarchy as operating system

This logic functioned in an era of:

stability
predictability
linearity
low complexity
slow change

That era has passed.

The world now behaves less like a machine
and more like a living system:

dynamic
interconnected
nonlinear
emergent
relational
continuously evolving

A machine struggles inside an ecosystem.

Organizations, too, strain when they try to operate with metaphors that no longer fit the world they inhabit.

The machine metaphor constrains organizations in predictable ways:

**Humans become functions:**
Valued for utility rather than potential.

**Creativity becomes an exception**:
Because machines cannot generate emergence.

**Decision-making centralizes**:
Because machines require a controller.

**Change is forced**:
Rather than allowed to unfold.

**Complexity overwhelms structure**:
Because machines break under load.

**Emotional and intuitive intelligence recede**:
Because depth is not required for mechanical output.

The outcomes are familiar:
burnout becomes systemic
innovation narrows
leadership turns performative
culture feels artificial
collaboration becomes political
coherence dissolves

These are not leadership failures.

They are signals that the metaphor itself has reached its limit.

When the metaphor shifts, a different organization becomes visible

An organization can be sensed as a living ecosystem that:
- breathe
- grow
- adapt
- evolve
- self-organize
- respond to conditions
- form and dissolve structure naturally
- hold multiple forms of intelligence at once
- operate through resonance rather than control

This is not a surface change.

It alters the foundation of organizational life.

In machine-based organizations, leadership enforces control.

In ecosystem-oriented organizations, leadership cultivates coherence.

Coherence arises through:
- shared resonance with what is being created
- alignment of human potential
- clarity of purpose
- relational integrity
- intuitive synchrony
- embodied presence

Coherence is not managed.

It is felt.
When coherence is present:
- decisions clarify
- conflict softens
- innovation expands
- communication flows
- trust deepens

Leadership shifts from management
to relational attunement.

In rigid systems:
roles define people
job descriptions constrain contribution
hierarchy limits expression

In living ecosystems:
roles remain fluid
contribution follows resonance
people shift positions as the field evolves

An energetic position is not a title.

It is a relational function within the ecosystem.

Examples may include:
stabilizer
visionary
integrator
connector
clarifier
catalyst
listener
translator
holder
expander
People move naturally between these positions
as awareness deepens
and as what is emerging changes.

This fluidity dramatically increases adaptability.

Hierarchies tend to be brittle.

Distributed intelligence is fluid.

In living ecosystems:
- sensing is shared
- awareness moves laterally
- decisions emerge from the field
- leadership rotates
- power flows toward resonance
- direction is guided by what is emerging

Such organizations become:
- more adaptive
- more resilient
- more innovative
- more humane
- more coherent

Distributed intelligence is not chaos.

It is coherence without central control.

Machine-based organizations optimize for efficiency:
- faster
- cheaper
- predictable

Living ecosystems orient toward evolution:
- deeper
- truer
- more emergent

The guiding question shifts:

From
"How do we do the same thing faster?"
To
"What wants to emerge next?"

Metrics transform accordingly:
growth becomes developmental
value becomes emergent
strategy becomes adaptive
innovation becomes organic
structure becomes responsive

Organizations stop chasing indicators
and begin listening for direction.

In ecosystems, tasks still exist.

But they are no longer the core.

Meaning becomes central.

Contribution arises from:
resonance
alignment
purpose
potential
clarity

The effects are tangible:
creativity deepens
engagement strengthens
collaboration gains power
friction reduces
fulfillment increases

Meaning is not a benefit.

It becomes the operating logic.

Ecosystem-oriented organizations follow patterns observable in nature.

They tend to:

**Self-organize around ideas**

Ideas act as attractors.
People resonate with different aspects.
Structure forms from resonance, not authority.

**Grow fractally**

Patterns replicate across teams, partners, and communities without losing coherence.

**Maintain permeable boundaries**

Allowing collaboration, exchange, and ecosystemic intelligence.

**Evolve through sensing, not force**

By attending to what people, ideas, and the wider system require.

This produces less conflict,
greater fluidity,
and stronger alignment.

Organizations shape daily life.

When they shift, society shifts.

As organizations become ecosystems:

power decentralizes
creativity expands
work becomes humane
leadership transforms
burnout diminishes
innovation broadens

economic models evolve
political structures soften
human potential expands

Organizations begin to function as:
stabilizing fields
developmental spaces
platforms for creation
communities of coherence
nodes of distributed intelligence

What comes into view is a society organized around resonance rather than force.

Organizations are no longer factories of productivity.

They are becoming living ecosystems of human potential and emergent creation.

This shift reshapes:
how work is experienced
how leadership is practiced
how innovation unfolds
how collaboration feels
how society organizes

Organizations begin to resemble:
living beings
relational networks
emergent fields
distributed intelligences
catalysts of human evolution

…

## Building a Resonant Society

When organizations begin to function as living ecosystems,
something larger starts to move.

The structures of society …
economic, political, cultural, educational, relational …
begin to transform as well.

Society is not separate from how humans work, create, and relate.
It is the emergent result of the patterns we enact together.

When human potential becomes the foundation of creation,
and resonance becomes the organizing principle
in teams and organizations,
the logic of society itself begins to shift.

The question is no longer:

> **"How do we fix society?"**

It becomes:

> **"What kind of society naturally emerges
> when human potential becomes the core operating principle?"**

This chapter explores that transformation …
not as a utopia,
but as a natural consequence of how emergence works.

As individuals develop integrated awareness
and organizations evolve into resonant ecosystems,
the social fabric begins to reorganize:

- decision-making
- community structures
- innovation cycles
- economics
- education

governance
human relationships
cultural norms

This change is not imposed.

It emerges from below …
from how people live, work, create, and relate.

Societal transformation begins as lived behavior
long before it becomes visible as structure.

Many existing societal structures rest on familiar assumptions:

- Centralized authority
- Hierarchical power
- Linear planning and control
- Extractive economics
- Suppression of human depth
- Fragmented institutions
- Predictive governance
- Competition as default logic

These structures strain because:

- complexity outpaces planning
- innovation outpaces regulation
- people outgrow institutions
- creativity exceeds hierarchy
- consciousness moves beyond control
- human potential expands faster than structure

The resulting tension appears everywhere:

- political polarization
- social fragmentation
- economic instability
- mental health crises
- declining trust

cultural hostility
loss of meaning

These are not individual failures.

They are signals of a system built on assumptions
that no longer match human development.

When people, organizations, and ideas are viewed through resonance,
a different societal pattern becomes visible.

A resonant society functions
as a network of ecosystems
connected through coherence rather than control.

It is not:

- centralized
- hierarchical
- uniform
- top-down

It is:

- distributed
- relational
- emergent
- adaptive
- interconnected
- self-organizing

This mirrors patterns found in:

- biological systems
- ecological networks
- neural networks
- digital networks
- human intuition
- emergence itself

These patterns endure
because they are resilient, intelligent, and adaptive.

A resonant society does not need to be designed.

It emerges through recognizable dynamics.

**Human Potential as the Core Resource**
In such a society:
education develops awareness rather than obedience
work develops potential rather than productivity
leadership cultivates coherence rather than control
relationships deepen rather than transact

Human potential becomes the primary asset
across institutions and systems.

**Emergent Ideas as the Engine of Innovation**
Innovation is no longer planned.

It emerges.

Ideas arise from the opportunity field.
People resonate with them.
Ecosystems form around them.
Organizations adapt to support them.
Society adjusts as their influence grows.
Innovation becomes the expression of human potential,
not its exploitation.

**Distributed Ecosystems Replace Hierarchies**
Across domains … education, healthcare, governance, economics …
structures begin to shift:
from centralized control
to distributed intelligence.

Communities self-organize around emergent needs.

Institutions stop imposing solutions
and begin listening for what wants to be created.

Society becomes:
- more resilient
- more responsive
- more intelligent
- more humane

**Resonance-Based Decision Making**

In a resonant society:
- decisions are not forced
- they emerge from coherence

People sense:
- what feels aligned
- what feels true
- what holds clarity for the whole
- what carries future coherence

This is not vague intuition.

It is distributed intelligence.

Because decision-making is located in the field,
not in a single authority,
it scales naturally.

The result is decisions that are:
- wiser
- smoother
- more sustainable
- less conflicted

**Collective Emergence as Direction**

In a resonant society,
the future is not predicted or imposed.

It emerges.

Society becomes capable of sensing:

- where human evolution is moving
- what ideas want to be created
- what structures no longer serve
- what wants to dissolve
- what wants to arise

The future becomes a co-created space
between human potential and emergent ideas.

Early expressions of a resonant society are already visible:

- schools cultivating awareness
- communities self-organizing around resonance
- distributed and collaborative governance
- conflict resolving through awareness
- workplaces becoming developmental ecosystems
- healthcare integrating embodied and intuitive dimensions
- economic activity flowing through relational networks
- intuition becoming a trained capacity

These are not ideals.

They are early forms.

Older societal models are organized around fear:

- fear of chaos
- fear of uncertainty
- fear of human depth
- fear of losing control
- fear of emergence

Fear requires:
- force
- compliance
- hierarchy
- suppression
- rationalization
- emotional avoidance

In a resonant society,
fear gradually releases
because coherence replaces control.

Stability no longer depends on suppression.

It arises from integration.

Human potential becomes:
- the stabilizing force
- the innovator
- the guide
- the connective tissue
- the creative engine
- the relational field

This is how a society governs itself
without needing to dominate itself.

A resonant society is not imagined.

It is emerging through:
- the rise of human potential
- the evolution of organizations
- the appearance of new ideas
- the spread of distributed ecosystems
- increasing complexity
- the collapse of outdated structures
- the awakening of intuitive intelligence

What is unfolding does not need invention.

It needs recognition, language, and coherence.

…

## Leadership as Resonance Stewardship

In earlier eras, leadership was associated with:

authority
control
decision-making
direction-setting
problem-solving
performance management
incentives and discipline
occupying a higher hierarchical position

This form of leadership does not translate well into environments shaped by:

emergent ideas
distributed ecosystems
human potential
relational intelligence
intuitive guidance
integrated awareness
collective coherence

It struggles where adaptation is constant,
where intelligence is distributed,
and where creation arises from resonance rather than command.

A different understanding of leadership begins to surface:

Leadership can be sensed as the stewardship of resonance.

It is not:

a role
a position
a title
a power function

It is a relational, energetic capacity
that stabilizes, guides, and amplifies coherence within an ecosystem.

Traditional leadership mirrors the machine metaphor:

the leader controls
the system obeys
information flows upward
directives flow downward
pressure enforces compliance
hierarchy maintains order

This structure strains under emergence because:

**No single person can sense everything**
Emergence requires distributed awareness.

**The future cannot be predicted**
Complexity dissolves predictive control.

**Coherence cannot be forced**
It must be cultivated.

**Hierarchy creates bottlenecks**
Filtering slows emergence.

**Emotional and intuitive intelligence recede**
The very capacities needed for uncertainty are suppressed.

These are not personal failures.

They reveal a structural mismatch
between old leadership forms and current conditions.

In resonant ecosystems, leadership is less about what a person does and more about the state of the relational field that forms around them.

Leadership becomes visible through the capacity to:

hold coherence
stabilize emotional tension
sense emerging direction
clarify collective intuition
amplify alignment

listen beneath words
ground the field
attune to what wants to happen
allow emergence
protect the integrity of what is unfolding
create safety for growth
embody calm presence

Leadership shifts from control
to presence.

The leader is not above the field.
The leader is within it …
not as a power center,
but as a grounding point.

Resonance stewardship emerges through the integration of three capacities.

**Embodied Stewardship - Holding the field**
A resonant leader can:
stabilize emotional turbulence
hold complexity without collapsing
remain grounded in uncertainty
absorb tension without absorbing identity
regulate the energetic environment
model safety through nervous-system coherence

Presence alone begins to shift the field.
This is why some people calm a room
without saying anything.

Leadership here arises through embodiment,
not authority.

**Rational Stewardship - Making sense without forcing**
A resonant leader can:
- articulate what others feel but cannot yet name
- clarify complexity without reducing it
- give language to emergence
- frame ideas with precision
- create shared understanding
- hold structure without rigidifying it

Clarity creates coherence.
Coherence reveals direction.

This is rational intelligence in service of life,
not dominance.

**Intuitive Stewardship - Sensing what is coming**
A resonant leader can:
- perceive early signals
- sense misalignment before conflict forms
- feel the next movement of the idea
- track the trajectory of the ecosystem
- notice when resonance fades
- sense what wants to be created

This is leadership through intuitive intelligence,
not prediction or control.

In older models, leaders were expected to speak first and most.

In resonant systems, leadership begins with listening.

Listening to:
- the idea
- the people involved
- the relational field
- the organization

the ecosystem
the future as it approaches
oneself

Leadership becomes quiet receptivity,
not performance.

The first responsibility is not to impose vision
or define strategy,
but to hear what is already forming.

Emergence carries intensity.

A resonant leader stabilizes the system by:
normalizing tension
allowing uncertainty
softening fear
grounding collective energy
holding space for growth
sensing when pressure becomes distortion
creating psychological and emotional safety

They do not avoid discomfort.
They metabolize it.

They do not push people to grow.
They help people feel safe enough to grow.

This mirrors nature's way of evolving.

Every emergent idea carries:
a direction
a rhythm
a pace
an inner coherence
a wisdom of its own

Resonant leadership protects this integrity by preventing:

rational pressure from distorting it
emotional fear from shrinking it
external expectation from overriding it
ego from hijacking it
urgency from accelerating it prematurely

The leader becomes a steward of emergence,
not an owner of the idea.

In resonant ecosystems, leadership is not centralized.

It becomes:

a shared capacity
a rotating function
a relational field

Different people lead at different moments,
depending on:

resonance
relevance
readiness
embodied state
clarity
intuitive alignment
relational position

Leadership becomes ubiquitous.
Hierarchy becomes unnecessary.

The ecosystem itself begins to lead.

A society organized around resonance
requires leaders who can:

steward coherence
hold complexity
listen deeply

navigate emergence
align human potential
protect new ideas
dissolve conflict
foster distributed intelligence
allow evolution without force

This form of leadership is not:

charismatic
dominant
controlling
performative
political

It is:

grounded
intuitive
relational
calm
deeply human

Such leaders do not rise by seeking power.

They become visible through coherence.

Leadership is recognized,
not declared.

Leadership in an emergent world is not an achievement.

It is a state.

A state of:

coherence
listening
resonance

attunement
presence
openness
humility
clarity
groundedness

Leadership becomes:
a stabilizing force
a relational intelligence
a field of awareness
a stewardship of emergence
a guardianship of ideas
a guide for human potential

…

## Power as Emergent Alignment

Every society, organization, and relationship is shaped by how power is understood.

In older systems, power was associated with:

control
dominance
authority
influence
leverage
hierarchy
the ability to enforce decisions

This form of power is finite.

If one person has more, another must have less.
It is rooted in fear, scarcity, and fragmentation.

In resonant ecosystems, this understanding begins to collapse.

It no longer reflects:

how creation happens
how human potential unfolds
how ideas emerge

A different form of power becomes visible …

not imposed,
not extracted,
not enforced,
not accumulated,
not weaponized,
not defended.

Power reveals itself as emergent alignment.

Traditional power systems rest on a small set of assumptions:

**People cannot be trusted** → control is required

**Intelligence must be centralized** → hierarchy is needed

**Conflict must be managed by force** → authority dominates

These assumptions generate predictable outcomes:
fear
compliance
suppression
distortion
disconnection
political maneuvering
low innovation
high burnout
systemic fragmentation

These are not side effects.

They are inherent properties of coercive power.

Such power cannot support:
emergence
intuition
creativity
relational intelligence
distributed sensing
collective alignment
human potential
ideas that want to be created

Control-based power suffocates emergence
because emergence requires freedom, coherence, and resonance.

In resonant ecosystems, power no longer operates *over* others.

It moves *through* alignment.

Through:

- coherence
- resonance
- collective intelligence
- emergent direction
- human potential

This power cannot be taken.
It cannot be forced.
It cannot be demanded.

It arises naturally
when the field becomes coherent.

Power becomes the energetic consequence of alignment.

In this mode:

- the idea carries power
- the field carries power
- coherence carries power
- emergence carries power
- the collective carries power

Power does not disappear.
It changes form.

When power is sensed as alignment, it appears as:

- clarity
- resonance
- embodied coherence
- intuitive precision
- relational trust
- emotional grounding
- the capacity to hold the field
- the ability to allow emergence
- influence through presence

People embodying this power do not require authority.

Their presence is sufficient.

This is why:
- some people calm a room without speaking
- some shift a conversation simply by arriving
- some stabilize conflict through grounded presence
- some create clarity with very few words
- some hold the emergent arc of an idea naturally

This is power that arises from *who someone is*,
not from what they can impose.

Power emerges when:
- A person is aligned with what is unfolding
- Embodied, rational, and intuitive layers are coherent
- Presence stabilizes the relational field
- Awareness matches what the moment requires
- Others sense safety, clarity, and direction through them

This alignment makes a person:
- trustworthy
- grounding
- resonant
- clear
- expansive
- integrative

People naturally orient toward coherence …
not because someone is "in charge,"
but because alignment is felt.

Emergent alignment draws attention
toward the source of coherence.

This is power.

When power is alignment:
anyone can access it
it expands without limit
one person's power strengthens another's
it becomes shared rather than hoarded
it circulates instead of accumulating

Old power is zero-sum.

Emergent power is positive-sum.

As alignment increases:
individual power grows
collective power amplifies
the field strengthens

Power becomes both:
distributed (everyone contributes)
amplified (the field grows as individuals grow)

Because it is not hierarchical,
it cannot be captured or controlled.

In resonant ecosystems, power is proportional to coherence.

More coherence → more power.
More fragmentation → less power.

Coherence arises through:
emotional grounding
intuitive clarity
rational precision
embodied presence
relational trust
resonance with the idea
alignment with the field

This explains why small, non-hierarchical groups often outperform large institutions.

Not because they are smarter …
but because they are more coherent.

Coherence is power.

In older systems, people fight for power because:

power is scarce
power controls resources
power determines safety
power enforces belonging

In resonant ecosystems:

power is abundant
power is emergent
power is shared
power circulates
power does not control belonging
power does not enforce compliance

The motivation for:

manipulation
dominance
competition
political games
hierarchical conflict

begins to dissolve.

People stop fighting for power
because power is no longer something
one person can possess.

It belongs to the field.

In older systems:
    leaders held power
    power created leaders
    hierarchy defined both

In resonant systems, these uncouple.

Leadership appears as resonance stewardship.
Power appears as emergent alignment.

A leader may or may not carry power …
it depends on coherence.

A person may carry power
without holding a formal leadership role.

Alignment is felt, not assigned.

Leadership becomes fluid.
Power becomes distributed.
The ecosystem holds both.

Perhaps the deepest shift is this:

**Power no longer requires control.**

Where older systems equated:
    power with domination
    safety with control
    identity with status
    influence with outcome management

Emergent systems reveal:
    power as alignment
    safety as coherence
    identity as resonance

This form of power:

empowers others
deepens trust
expands creativity
accelerates emergence
stabilizes uncertainty
aligns people with ideas
heals fragmentation

It is the opposite of dominance.

It is the embodiment of freedom.

In this emerging world, power appears as:

natural
fluid
emergent
relational
coherent
intuitive
grounded
abundant

No one needs to seize it.
No one needs to defend it.
No one needs to compete for it.

It emerges wherever alignment is strongest.
It amplifies human potential.
It supports emergence.
It heals fragmentation.

…

## Conflict as Insight, Not Opposition

Conflict is one of the most misunderstood forces in human life.

In older systems, conflict has been interpreted as:

- threat
- opposition
- misalignment
- error
- dysfunction
- breakdown
- something to be avoided, suppressed, or resolved through force

Conflict is treated as a problem …
a deviation from a desired state of harmony.

When viewed through emergence, human development, and resonant ecosystems,
this interpretation begins to dissolve.

Conflict is not a problem.

Conflict is information.

It signals:

- emerging change
- misalignment between layers of awareness
- subconscious patterns surfacing
- emotional truth seeking expression
- relational incoherence moving toward coherence
- ideas evolving faster than current capacity
- the field reorganizing itself
- the next developmental step becoming visible

Conflict becomes insight …
and insight becomes the entry point to growth.

Control-based systems fear conflict because their stability depends on:

- hierarchy
- fixed roles
- obedience
- predictability
- suppression of emotional truth
- avoidance of intuitive intelligence

Conflict threatens these structures because:

**It reveals what has been suppressed**
Control weakens when truth surfaces.

**It disrupts efficiency**
Mechanical systems cannot adapt to unpredictability.

**It introduces emotional complexity**
Systems built for output cannot hold embodied truth.

**It challenges authority**
Compliance is required for hierarchy to function.

**It exposes misalignment**
Stability is prioritized over coherence.

As a result, conflict is often:

- avoided
- punished
- silenced
- labeled unprofessional
- framed as weakness
- treated as failure

This produces familiar outcomes:

- resentment
- distrust
- passive aggression
- hidden power struggles

emotional shutdown
fragmentation
relational fractures

The system appears calm
while coherence quietly erodes.

This is the false peace of suppression.

When conflict is seen differently, its function becomes clear.

Conflict is not opposition.
Conflict is information.

It reveals:
where the field is shifting
where resonance is weakening
where subconscious patterns activate
where emotional truth seeks voice
where rational clarity is missing
where intuitive direction is evolving
where growth is required
where ideas invite change

Conflict is not a disruption to coherence.

It is the pathway to deeper coherence.

It is the system showing what wants to be integrated next.

Emergence is knocking.

Conflict tends to appear when:

**Layers of awareness - embodied, rational, intuitive - are misaligned**
Within a person or between people.

**An idea evolves faster than current capacity**
Creating tension between old patterns and new direction.

**Subconscious material surfaces**
Requesting recognition and integration.

**Relational coherence weakens**
Revealing unresolved emotional dynamics.

**The field reorganizes itself**
Requiring shifts in roles, positions, or perspectives.

**Collective intelligence tries to communicate**
Before conscious understanding is available.

In every case, conflict is a signal … not dysfunction.

It is intelligence arriving ahead of language.

In resonant ecosystems, conflict is not solved.

It is integrated.

Older systems escalate.
Resonant systems slow.

Slowing reveals:
the truth beneath tension
the wisdom inside emotional charge
the pattern being activated
the misaligned layer of awareness
the next evolutionary step

Slowness transforms conflict into clarity.

Resonant systems attend to:
　　what the body is signaling
　　what the mind is articulating
　　what intuition is sensing

When all three are heard,
the full picture emerges.

Most conflict is partial truth
colliding with another partial truth.

Integration dissolves charge.

In older systems, emotions are threats.

In resonant systems, emotions are messages.

The charge is not the problem.
Unintegrated meaning is.

When emotional truth is held …
not judged, suppressed, or acted out …
it reorganizes naturally.

This is how conflict transforms.

Every conflict hides something deeper:
　　a longing
　　a fear
　　an alignment
　　a truth seeking coherence

When this deeper resonance is recognized,
the surface conflict loses intensity
and becomes guidance.

Conflict is not resolved.

It is absorbed.

The system updates:
coherence
relationships
structure
shared understanding

Conflict becomes evolution.

When met directly, conflict becomes:
a moment of awakening
an opportunity for repair
a signal of the next growth edge
a point of recalibration
a window into deeper truth
a strengthening force
a pathway to higher coherence

Tension gives way to trust.
Friction gives way to clarity.
Rupture gives way to alignment.

Conflict becomes catalyst …
not breakdown.

Suppressed conflict:
fragments systems
erodes trust
dulls intuition
collapses coherence
distorts emergence
destabilizes the field
blocks growth

Invisible damage accumulates.

Suppression harms far more
than open, integrated conflict.

When a system can no longer tell itself the truth,
it loses the capacity to evolve.

Truth is the oxygen of resonant ecosystems.

Conflict does not appear randomly.

It arrives precisely
when the system is ready to evolve.

It reveals:
  the next layer of coherence
  the next developmental step
  the next structural adjustment
  the next movement of the idea
  the next truth required for alignment

Conflict is emergence
pressing against the limits of current form.

When met, those limits expand.
When resisted, the system contracts.

In resonant ecosystems and societies,
conflict ceases to be:
  threat
  disruption
  breakdown
  opposition
  failure

It becomes:

insight
intelligence
clarity
growth
evolution
emergence
truth
coherence

Conflict becomes organizing intelligence …
keeping systems alive, adaptive, and aligned.

…

## Relationships as Resonant Fields

Relationships are the invisible architecture of human life.

They shape:

- emotional landscapes
- identity
- intuition
- creativity
- sense of safety
- capacity to grow
- ability to perceive emergence

A deeper truth becomes visible:

> Relationships are not interactions between individuals.
> They are shared resonance fields.

Within these fields:

- embodied patterns meet
- rational worlds intersect
- intuitive signals intertwine
- subconscious truth surfaces
- emotional reality becomes visible
- ideas move between people
- growth activates
- coherence forms or dissolves
- potential expands or contracts

A relationship is not what two people say to each other.

A relationship is the dynamic that lives between them.

When this becomes visible, relationships can be seen as the foundation of:

resonant societies
resonant organizations
resonant creation

Most people grow within relational systems shaped by:

attachment wounds
emotional suppression
fixed roles and expectations
unconscious coping patterns
the need for approval
fear of conflict
avoidance of truth
power imbalance
rational negotiation
emotional compromise
unintegrated trauma

As a result, many relationships are built on survival rather than resonance.

Survival-based relationships tend to:

manage tension instead of exploring it
negotiate needs instead of understanding them
oscillate between closeness and avoidance
rely on agreements to mask emotional chaos
confuse peace with suppression
use control or withdrawal for stability
repeat inherited patterns rather than emerging truth

These dynamics limit human potential
because they cannot hold emergence.

They enforce stability rather than coherence.

This is why people often feel:
drained
unseen
misunderstood
unsafe
disconnected
over-attached
exhausted
confused

The issue is not individual failure.

It is fragmentation in the relational field.

When seen differently, relationships take on a new character.

A relationship can be sensed as a shared resonance field
in which two or more people respond to each other
across embodied, rational, and intuitive awareness.

This means:
the body responds to embodied truth
the mind interprets and clarifies shared meaning
intuition senses what the relationship is becoming

This is why resonant relationships feel alive:
energy flows
presence deepens
direction appears
truth emerges
growth unfolds naturally

Resonant relationships do not require effort.

They require awareness.

Relationships deepen when all three layers are present.

**Embodied Resonance**
*Nervous system to nervous system*

This layer senses:
- safety or threat
- tension or openness
- suppression or availability
- excitement or fear
- unspoken truth
- unresolved patterns

Embodied resonance forms the foundation.

Without it:
- communication fragments
- trust erodes
- intuition distorts
- rational clarity collapses

This is why people can say all the right things
and still feel disconnected.

**Rational Resonance**
*Shared meaning*

This layer includes:
- shared language
- shared interpretation
- shared understanding
- shared context

Rational resonance is not agreement.

It is coherence of meaning.

Without it:
assumptions multiply
defensiveness grows
misunderstanding escalates
conflict hardens

Rational resonance stabilizes the relationship
but does not animate it.

That role belongs to intuition.

**Intuitive Resonance**
*Shared sensing of becoming*

This layer perceives:
direction
vitality
unfolding potential
deeper purpose

Intuitive resonance allows relationships to:
move through conflict
navigate uncertainty
grow through complexity
evolve with meaning

Without intuitive resonance, relationships stagnate.

When embodied, rational, and intuitive resonance align,
relationships enter a fourth state:

**Emergent relational intelligence**
This feels like:
effortless understanding
deep recognition
shared direction

mutual growth
intuitive clarity
emotional truth
a sense of something larger moving through the connection

These are the relationships that:
change lives
ignite ideas
shape ecosystems
transform societies

The relational field becomes a source of:
creativity
healing
insight
shared purpose
collective evolution

This is resonance made relational.

**Conflict in Resonant Relationships**
As seen earlier, conflict is insight.

In resonant relationships, conflict appears as:
relational truth surfacing
emotional depth seeking expression
subconscious patterns asking for integration
intuition signaling a next step
the relationship evolving itself
the field adjusting
Conflict is not a rupture of connection.

It is the doorway to the next level of connection.

In resonant relationships:

- truth is spoken without collapse
- emotion surfaces without fear
- ideas emerge without competition
- intuition is shared
- misalignment becomes guidance
- boundaries clarify
- connection expands

These relationships do not avoid tension.

They recognize tension as transformation beginning.

They do not cling to identity.

They allow identity to evolve.

They do not collapse into reactivity
because embodied awareness remains grounded.

A resonant society cannot rest on:

- suppressed emotion
- authoritarian structures
- fragmented relational fields
- fear-based dynamics
- rational-only communication

A resonant society requires:

- emotionally coherent relationships
- shared intuitive sensing
- rational clarity
- relational safety
- distributed intelligence
- integrated conflict
- emergent alignment

Society is built through relationships.
Relationships are built through resonance.

Relationships are not merely personal.

They are structural.

They are the medium through which:

- ideas take form
- human potential expands
- ecosystems grow
- leadership emerges
- power circulates
- conflict transforms
- society evolves

When relationships are grounded in resonance,
the world organizes itself around resonance.

…

## Communities as Coherent Fields of Belonging

Communities are not collections of people.

They are shared resonance fields that hold:

belonging
identity
safety
meaning
creation
evolution

A community is not defined by:

geography
shared interests
shared goals
shared identity
shared culture

These are surface expressions.

The deeper reality is this:

A community is a coherent field
that shapes how people come into being together.

When coherence is present, a community feels:

safe
alive
meaningful
nourishing
purposeful
expansive

When coherence fragments, the field feels:

- tense
- chaotic
- polarized
- rigid
- suppressive
- disconnected

Communities are not built through structure.

They are formed through coherence.

This chapter explores how communities evolve
when resonance becomes the organizing principle
and human potential becomes the foundation of belonging.

Traditional communities formed around:

- geography (villages, towns, schools)
- identity (religion, nationality, profession)
- roles (family systems, organizations)
- shared survival needs
- shared obligations
- conformity
- group norms
- authority structures

These forms worked when:

- life was local
- change was slow
- identities were fixed
- obedience ensured stability
- institutions defined meaning
- survival required conformity

They strain now because:

- life is global
- change is rapid
- identities are fluid
- intuition is awakening
- human potential is rising
- belonging is no longer inherited
- meaning is no longer imposed
- people outgrow suppressive structures

The old model is breaking.

Not because community is disappearing,
but because community is evolving.

Resonant communities do not form around:

- belief
- ideology
- identity
- location
- obligation

They form around:

- coherence
- resonance
- human potential
- the idea that wants to be created between people

A resonant community becomes visible when:

- people feel seen
- people feel grounded
- people feel safe to express truth
- people feel aligned with the field
- collective intuition opens
- shared emergence becomes perceptible
- growth becomes mutual

The community is experienced as a living ecosystem …
not a structure, but a field.

Just as individuals and relationships resonate across three layers, communities also develop coherence through:

**Embodied Coherence**
*The collective nervous system*

A community with embodied coherence feels:
safe
grounded
present
relationally open

People can:
relax
speak truth
disagree
be vulnerable
show emotion
hold others' emotions
sense the field

This is the opposite of:
social anxiety
groupthink
suppression
performance
unspoken tension

Embodied coherence is the foundation
of all healthy community.

**Rational Coherence**
*The shared meaning field*

A resonant community shares:
language
concepts
stories
understanding
direction

Not enforced …
but emerging naturally from the field.

Rational coherence allows a community to:
make sense of itself
hold shared clarity
navigate complexity
articulate its evolution
orient toward change

It is not uniformity.

It is shared meaning
that supports individuality.

**Intuitive Coherence**
*Shared sensing of becoming*

This layer carries:
purpose
momentum
direction
creativity
emergence

It appears as:
collective insight
spontaneous alignment
shared intuition
group flow
emergent strategy
unexpected clarity
a felt sense of "this is where we are going"

When intuitive coherence is present,
communities evolve naturally.

When embodied, rational, and intuitive coherence converge,
the community enters a new state:

**Collective emergence.**

In this state:
ideas accelerate
creativity expands
new roles form effortlessly
conflict integrates quickly
innovation arises from unexpected places
leadership rotates fluidly
people step into their potential
the community becomes generative

Such communities feel alive
in ways older societal structures cannot replicate.

They are early expressions
of a resonant society.
Resonant communities tend to have:
porous boundaries
fluid participation
open dialogue

emotional safety
intuitive clarity
distributed leadership
integrated conflict
clear relational fields
alignment with ideas that want to be created

They can be found in:
deep startup teams
embodied leadership circles
resonance-based groups
communities of practice
artistic and creative collectives
entrepreneurial ecosystems
relationally-aware families
intentional organizations

These communities grow through coherence,
not scale.

In resonant communities, conflict becomes:
a learning moment
a generator of clarity
a field recalibration
a signal of evolving direction
an opportunity to integrate deeper truth

Instead of fracturing the group:
conflict strengthens coherence
sides dissolve into understanding
tension reorganizes the field
The community grows *through* conflict,
not despite it.

A resonant community evolves through:
emergent leadership
shifting roles
expanding or contracting boundaries
new ideas entering the field
old structures dissolving
deeper levels of coherence
new relational patterns
increasing complexity
intuitive guidance

Movement occurs like a living organism …
through collective sensing rather than control.

A resonant community is not a refuge from growth.

It is a container for growth.

It holds a field for
human potential
emergent ideas
relational evolution
distributed intelligence
intuitive clarity
emotional truth
societal transformation

Resonant communities become
the living infrastructure of a resonant society.

They are the social units
through which emergence scales.
Older communities offer belonging when:
identity matches
rules are followed
norms are obeyed

differences are suppressed
loyalty overrides truth

Resonant communities offer belonging when:
potential is seen
truth is welcome
intuition is valued
growth is supported
contribution matters
awareness expands
alignment strengthens

Belonging becomes resonance,
not a role.

This is the foundation
of a new social fabric.

In a resonant society, communities become:
coherent fields
generative ecosystems
relational organisms
developmental spaces
containers for emergence
incubators for ideas
catalysts for evolution

They are not made of people alone.
They are made of resonance.

…

## Institutions of the Emergent World

Institutions are the structural memory of society.

They carry roles, responsibilities, and agreements across generations.
They hold continuity for:

- governance
- education
- justice
- economics
- public services
- health
- infrastructure
- collective identity

But the institutions we inherited were designed for a world that no longer exists.

They were built for:

- stability
- predictability
- slow change
- centralized power
- obedience
- hierarchy
- mechanical efficiency
- rational control
- uniformity

They cannot hold the complexity, speed, and fluidity
of an emergent society grounded in human potential.

The mismatch produces the global tensions we see today.

Institutional crisis is not a failure of people.
It is a failure of structure.

This chapter explores how institutions evolve
when resonance, coherence, and distributed intelligence
become the foundation of societal organization.

Older institutions strain because they are:

**Built on hierarchy**
Centralized authority cannot process distributed intelligence.
It becomes a bottleneck under complexity.

**Built on predictability**
Modern systems are nonlinear and emergent.
Structures optimized for stability cannot respond to constant change.

**Built on obedience**
Human potential can no longer be compressed into fixed roles.
Creativity, awareness, and intuition exceed institutional boundaries.

**Built on rational control**
Emergence requires emotional, embodied, and intuitive intelligence.
Institutions suppress exactly the capacities now required.

**Built on uniformity**
A fluid, interconnected society requires adaptability, not conformity.

**Built on scarcity**
Modern ecosystems operate through abundance of creativity,
not scarcity of power.

**Built on authority rather than resonance**
Authority erodes trust.
Resonance generates it.

Old institutions are collapsing not because they are obsolete,
but because the patterns they operate on
are incompatible with human evolution.

In a resonant society, institutions do not disappear.

They transform.

They shift from rigid structures
to dynamic ecosystems that:

- sense the field
- respond to emergence
- distribute intelligence
- support human potential
- protect coherence
- hold long-term agreements
- adapt fluidly
- evolve naturally
- listen deeply
- facilitate creation

These institutions are not built on control.

They are built on alignment.

Not hierarchy → resonance.
Not stability → adaptability.
Not authority → coherence.

They become stabilizing forces
in a world shaped by emergence.

Emergent institutions operate across the same tri-level structure
introduced earlier in the book.

### Embodied Institutions

*Stabilizing the collective nervous system*

These institutions:

- create psychological and emotional safety
- cultivate trust
- hold relational coherence
- support human wellbeing
- regulate social tension
- integrate conflict
- reduce societal fragmentation

Examples include:

- community-based justice models
- trauma-informed public services
- relational healthcare systems
- restorative conflict practices

Their focus is not enforcement,
but restoring coherence.

### Rational Institutions

*Holding structure without rigidity*

These institutions:

- articulate shared purpose
- codify agreements
- define roles and boundaries
- steward resources
- ensure fairness
- maintain continuity

Their structures remain flexible and adaptive.
They are frameworks, not cages.

Examples include:

distributed governance models
adaptive policy frameworks
transparent resource flows
dynamic regulatory ecosystems
community-defined decision processes

They provide stability … without suppressing emergence.

**Intuitive Institutions**

*Sensing societal becoming*

These institutions:

detect emergent direction
sense collective intuition
listen into what wants to be created
identify new possibilities
hold space for innovation
adapt to emerging truth

They function as a collective sensing layer
for societal evolution.

Examples include:

idea incubation fields
cultural sensing networks
research ecosystems
foresight collectives
cross-sector resonance fields

Their role is not prediction,
but guidance through awareness.

When embodied, rational, and intuitive institutions align,
a new capacity appears:

**Collective emergent governance.**

This form of governance is not:

political
ideological
centralized
force-based

It is:

relational
distributed
intuitive
adaptive
coherent

Governance becomes the nervous system of society,
not its enforcement mechanism.

Emergent institutions tend to share common patterns:

**Distributed intelligence**
Decisions emerge from coherent fields, not authority figures.

**Permeable boundaries**
Institutions collaborate fluidly with communities and ecosystems.

**Dynamic structure**
Roles and rules adapt as the field evolves.

**Conflict integration**
Tension becomes insight rather than opposition.

**Resonance before action**
Direction is sensed, not imposed.

**Human potential as resource**
Development replaces obedience.

**Idea-driven evolution**
Institutions grow around ideas that want to be created.

These patterns produce institutions that are:

- humane
- innovative
- adaptive
- stable
- aligned with human development
- aligned with emergence

Early forms of emergent institutions are already appearing:

- restorative justice communities
- regenerative agriculture networks
- distributed governance ecosystems
- collaborative research collectives
- participatory budgeting models
- relational healthcare systems
- citizen assemblies
- decentralized cultural movements
- self-organizing education circles

These are not anomalies.
They are early signals
of a new institutional era.

A resonant society does not dissolve into chaos.

Human systems still require:

- structure
- agreements
- continuity
- containers
- collective memory
- stewardship of shared resources

Emergent institutions provide these
without suppressing emergence.

They create:
structure without rigidity
stability without control
continuity without stagnation

They serve the system
rather than dominating it.

In a resonant society, institutions evolve from:

| | | |
|---|---|---|
| authority | → | coherence |
| control | → | alignment |
| enforcement | → | relational integration |
| rules | → | adaptive principles |
| hierarchy | → | distributed intelligence |
| uniformity | → | flexibility |
| resistance | → | responsiveness |

Institutions become:
alive
relational
intuitive
developmental
fluid
self-correcting

This is not reform.

It is reinvention.

Institutions cease to be:
bottlenecks
blockers
rigid containers

And become:
facilitators
amplifiers
guardians of coherence

Institutions of the emergent world:
sense the field
adapt continuously
hold coherence
cultivate human potential
distribute power
integrate conflict
support resonant communities
evolve with ideas
respond to emergence

They allow society to become:
more alive
more resilient
more humane
more innovative
more aligned with consciousness

…

## The Economics of Resonance

Every society is shaped by its economic foundation.

The industrial world was shaped by:

extraction
productivity
efficiency
competition
scarcity
centralized capital
hierarchical organizations
transactional value

This economic logic built the world we know …
and the world we are now outgrowing.

Human potential is rising.
Ideas want to be created.
Emergence is accelerating.
Institutions are shifting.
Work is becoming developmental.
Communities are becoming resonant.
Leadership is becoming stewardship.
Power is becoming alignment.

Economics cannot remain the same.

A different economic logic is becoming visible …
one that reflects the nature of:

complexity
distributed intelligence
human potential
relational coherence

emergent ideas
resonance fields
ecosystems
intuition

What comes into view can be recognized as
**the economics of resonance.**

The old economic system strains because it rests on assumptions that no longer match lived reality.

**Scarcity as the foundation**
Yet human creativity is abundant, not scarce.

**Productivity as the measure of value**
Yet the highest-value contributions are relational, intuitive, and emergent.

**Labor as a traded commodity**
Yet human potential cannot be reduced to hours.

**Hierarchical organization of value creation**
Yet value increasingly emerges from distributed networks.

**Capital concentration as the engine of growth**
Yet future growth arises from collective resonance.

**Competitive pressure as the source of innovation**
Yet the deepest innovations arise from coherence, not conflict.

**Risk as unpredictable randomness**
Yet risk reveals itself as developmental … the capacity to grow with an idea.

**Wealth as accumulation**
Yet in resonance-based systems, wealth appears as expansion of potential,
not accumulation of resources.

The mismatch between economic logic and human reality is widening.

The system does not feel broken.
It feels exhausted.

Not failing … becoming obsolete.

In a resonance-based world, value is not created by:

- productivity
- efficiency
- scarcity
- extraction

Value emerges from:

- alignment
- coherence
- potential
- creation
- connection
- emergence

Value becomes that which:

- increases the capacity of individuals to access their human potential
- increases the coherence of relationships
- strengthens the resonance of communities
- enhances the intelligence of ecosystems
- enables ideas to manifest
- supports the evolution of the whole field

This marks a shift
from **transactional value**
to **emergent value**.

In the old system:

| | | |
|---|---|---|
| value | = | labor + capital |
| humans | = | resources |
| work | = | output |
| growth | = | more of the same |

In a resonance-based economy:

Human potential becomes the primary economic asset.

Human potential generates:

creativity
intuition
insight
innovation
relational intelligence
conflict integration
emotional truth
coherence
emergent solutions

These become the true sources of value
in a world defined by complexity and emergence.

Human potential is not a resource.

It is the generative engine of the economy.

In older systems:

ideas must prove themselves
investors select them
resources are allocated through risk-return logic
ideas compete for survival

In a resonance-based economy:
    ideas that want to be created pull resources toward themselves

Ideas become:
    attractors
    organizers
    economic agents
    energizing nodes
    coherence generators

Instead of competing for capital,
ideas organize capital.

Instead of proving their worth,
ideas reveal their value through coherence and alignment.

Innovation shifts from selection
to recognition.

In the conventional startup economy:
    most companies fail
    a few outliers repay the portfolio
    investment relies on probability
    uncertainty is managed through pressure

This model follows directly
from misunderstanding how ideas emerge.

When risk is seen differently,
a simple insight appears:

Risk does not sit in the idea.
Risk sits in the ecosystem's capacity
to grow with the idea.

Risk becomes:
developmental
relational
systemic
embodied
intuitive

And because resonance-based ecosystems
are designed to grow with ideas,
risk becomes lower, more predictable, and manageable.

Capital begins to flow differently.

Resonant capital flows toward:
coherence
potential
alignment
resonance
emergent clarity
relational integrity
ideas with inherent wisdom

Capital becomes a follower, not a leader.

It follows:
resonance
human potential
emergent ideas

The old logic reverses:
capital no longer selects ideas
ideas attract capital

Capital becomes a nutrient,
not a gatekeeper.

In older economies:
value is traded
labor is purchased
money mediates everything
efficiency maximizes profit

In resonance-based economies:
exchange becomes contribution

People contribute:
potential
creativity
presence
awareness
growth
coherence
emergent insight

Money still exists …
but meaning flows before money flows.

Value appears as:
mutual expansion
mutual coherence
mutual emergence

Exchange becomes generative,
not extractive.

In older systems:
wealth = accumulation
power = resource control
status = capital advantage

In a resonance-based economy:
wealth appears as expanded human potential
and the coherence of ecosystems

A wealthy society is one where:
people can grow
relationships are safe
ideas can emerge
communities are coherent
institutions are adaptive
ecosystems are alive
creativity flows freely

This is wealth as:
flourishing
generativity
resonance
possibility
expansion

As this economic logic unfolds, new structures emerge naturally:
regenerative startups
idea-centric investment ecosystems
human-potential-based compensation
distributed governance networks
contribution-based economies
resonance-driven resource allocation
emergent project teams
adaptive public institutions
community-based development
ecosystems of collective intelligence

The economic landscape shifts:

| | | |
|---|---|---|
| competition | → | collaboration |
| scarcity | → | abundance |
| accumulation | → | contribution |
| extraction | → | regeneration |
| control | → | alignment |
| prediction | → | emergence |

This is not incremental reform.

It is a foundational transition.

The economics of resonance:
unlocks human potential
aligns creation with emergence
transforms money into an enabler
reduces systemic risk
decentralizes power
amplifies creativity
supports coherent communities
guides institutional evolution
nurtures ideas that want to be created

This economic order does not need to be imposed.

It emerges naturally
when human potential and resonance
become the foundation of society.

…

## Measuring What Truly Matters

Measurement shapes behavior.
It shapes decisions.
It shapes systems.
It shapes society.

What is measured becomes what is valued.
And what is valued becomes what is built.

In the industrial world, measurement was designed for:

efficiency
productivity
output
reduction of complexity
control
predictability
comparison
competition

These measurements produced familiar indicators:

GDP as the measure of national health
quarterly revenue as the measure of business value
standardized tests as the measure of intelligence
productivity as the measure of worker worth
utilization as the measure of economic efficiency
ROI as the measure of investment success
KPIs as the measure of organizational alignment

Yet these metrics do not measure:

human potential
relational coherence
collective intelligence
emotional well-being
idea emergence
resonance
systemic health

intuitive clarity
meaning
creativity
adaptability
distributed awareness

They cannot …
because they were designed to measure machines, not living systems.

A resonant society requires a different relationship with measurement.
One aligned with human development, emergence, coherence,
and the evolution of awareness itself.

Conventional metrics distort the world because they:

**Reduce complexity to single numbers**
Erasing nuance and living intelligence.

**Count only what can be controlled**
Ignoring what actually drives evolution.

**Incentivize short-term extraction**
At the cost of long-term coherence.

**Impose uniformity**
Despite human diversity and relational complexity.

**Reward suppression**
Because emotional truth is not considered "productive."

**Punish growth**
Because growth often begins as disruption.

**Hide the cost of fragmentation**
Because disconnection is difficult to quantify.

**Ignore emergence**
Because they measure only what has already happened,
not what is becoming possible.

These metrics blind systems
to the very capacities needed to navigate a complex world.

A society guided by outdated measurements
cannot evolve coherently.

A different orientation toward measurement becomes visible:

What matters is not output …
but capacity.

Capacity is the ability to:
- sense
- grow
- adapt
- cohere
- create
- align
- relate
- integrate conflict
- follow emergence

Output measures the past.
Capacity reflects the future.

Capacity reveals whether a system can meet
what is trying to emerge next.

A resonant world naturally begins to attend to five interconnected dimensions.

**Human Potential Capacity**
*The ability of individuals to grow and evolve*

This becomes visible through:
- emotional coherence
- intuitive access
- relational awareness
- ability to navigate uncertainty

developmental movement
embodied presence
cognitive clarity
creative flow
adaptability

This reflects flourishing …
not performance.

**Relational Field Health**
*The quality of the connections holding the system*

This is sensed through:
conflict integration
emotional truthfulness
mutual resonance
trust
openness
clarity
shared direction
attunement

Relationships become infrastructure.

**Ecosystem Coherence**
*The intelligence of the whole system*

This appears as:
distributed intelligence
community coherence
leadership fluidity
idea alignment
systemic adaptability
boundary permeability
sensing accuracy
collective intuition

Ecosystems become the unit of organizational health.

**Idea Emergence and Realization**
*How ideas that want to be created come into form*

This becomes visible through:
- idea clarity
- resonance strength
- ecosystem alignment
- pace of emergence
- degree of manifestation
- coherence of unfolding
- depth of impact

Ideas become active indicators of systemic intelligence.

**Societal Flourishing**
*The overall health of the collective field*

This is sensed through:
- reduced fragmentation
- increased relational safety
- collective adaptability
- institutional coherence
- emergence of new ideas
- distribution of opportunity
- well-being beyond happiness metrics
- reduction of suppression
- expansion of human potential

Flourishing becomes the measure of civilization.

Traditional KPIs focus on performance and control.

A resonant system begins to notice different signals … signals of alignment and coherence.

These may include indicators such as:

field coherence
conflict integration capacity
leadership resonance
clarity of collective intuition
idea attractor strength
community resilience
human potential growth
responsiveness to emergence

These are not abstractions.

They can be sensed and observed through:

behavioral patterns
relational dynamics
decision-making quality
language use
group flow states
idea evolution
ecosystem health

The science of such measurement is still emerging, but the direction is already clear.

A resonant society does not abandon measurement.

It transforms its role.

Measurement becomes:

awareness
reflection
feedback
coherence mapping
developmental guidance
relational understanding
collective sensing

Measurement ceases to be a tool of control
and becomes an instrument of evolution.

As this shift unfolds, certain measurements lose relevance:

productivity per hour
obedience
compliance
forced efficiency
standardized performance
output without context
competitive ranking
zero-sum success

These metrics collapse human potential.
They belong to a world that is passing.

Attention naturally turns toward:

aliveness
alignment
emergence
developmental movement
ecosystem health
relational coherence
intuitive clarity
creative innovation
systemic integrity

Measurement begins to reflect life
rather than extraction.

In the emergent world:

we measure what matters
we notice capacity, not output
we attend to coherence, not control
we sense emergence, not prediction
we value flourishing, not productivity

we recognize resonance, not ranking
we see systems as living ecosystems, not machines

Measurement becomes the mirror
through which a system perceives itself …
not to judge,
but to grow.

…

## Learning as Becoming

Learning is not the acquisition of knowledge.
Learning is the evolution of consciousness.

Development is not the accumulation of skills.
Development is the expansion of awareness.

Human potential is not talent waiting to be unlocked.
Human potential is the natural expression of the tri-level human
when the environment becomes coherent enough
for emergence to unfold.

In the old system, learning was:

- linear
- hierarchical
- standardized
- rational
- externally driven
- authority-controlled
- performance-evaluated
- disconnected from intuition
- disconnected from embodiment
- disconnected from meaning
- disconnected from real human development

This system no longer works
because it was designed for yesterday's human,
not the human that is emerging now.

This chapter explores how learning evolves
when tri-level awareness, resonance, coherence, and emergence
become the living principles of development.

For centuries, education served the needs of institutions, not people.

Its purpose was to:
  produce obedient workers
  teach compliance
  train rational thinking devoid of intuition
  suppress emotional truth
  standardize knowledge
  fit humans into roles
  maintain societal order
  reinforce authority
  punish deviation
  reward conformity

In this system:
  creativity is optional
  intuition is irrelevant
  emotions are dangerous
  embodiment is ignored
  truth is external
  learning is passive
  intelligence is measured by recall
  growth is linear
  developmental needs are suppressed
  human potential is constrained
  knowing replaces awareness

This model is collapsing
because it cannot support the kind of human
the future now requires.

In a resonant world, learning is not about:
  content
  curriculum
  achievement
  ranking
  credentials

Learning becomes:
- the expansion of human potential
- the integration of embodied, rational, and intuitive awareness
- the ability to sense and co-create with emergence

Learning becomes:
- developmental
- relational
- intuitive
- embodied
- emergent
- creative
- iterative
- experiential
- reflective
- integrated
- meaningful

The orientation shifts
from **knowing more**
to **becoming more**.

Human development unfolds through the integration of three layers of awareness.

**Embodied Learning**
Learning through the nervous system, emotion, and lived experience.

This includes:
- somatic awareness
- emotional literacy
- nervous-system coherence
- trauma integration
- embodied presence
- regulation in complexity
- intuitive sensing through the body

Embodied learning is foundational.

Without it, development collapses
into performance, reactivity, and control.

**Rational Learning**
Learning through clarity, structure, and conceptual understanding.

This includes:
- critical thinking
- systems thinking
- language and metaphor
- meaning-making
- analytical reasoning
- abstraction and structure
- reflective understanding

Rational learning organizes experience.

It shapes and clarifies,
but does not dominate.

**Intuitive Learning**
Learning through resonance, insight, and emergent direction.

This includes:
- sensing the field
- recognizing ideas that want to be created
- hearing deeper truth
- perceiving alignment
- acting from resonance
- following emergent clarity
- stepping into the unknown
- trusting intuitive intelligence

Intuitive learning is where the future becomes visible.

When embodied, rational, and intuitive learning integrate,
a new capacity appears:

**Emergent intelligence** …
the ability to navigate uncertainty, complexity, and transformation
with coherence and clarity.

This intelligence:
- sees patterns others miss
- perceives opportunities before they become obvious
- moves with emergence rather than resisting it
- creates new frameworks rather than repeating old ones
- elevates conflict into insight
- strengthens relational coherence
- enables ideas to take form

This intelligence is not taught.
It emerges when the environment allows it.

In a resonant world, development is not:
- performance improvement
- skills acquisition
- productivity enhancement
- compliance with norms

Development becomes:
- the expansion of the human system's capacity
- to hold complexity, truth, resonance, and emergence

This expansion unfolds across:
- emotional capacity
- relational capacity
- intuitive capacity
- cognitive capacity

embodied capacity
creative capacity
conflict capacity
systemic capacity

As capacity expands:
contribution increases naturally
intuition clarifies
presence grounds
ideas sharpen
relationships cohere
leadership emerges
work gains meaning
life aligns

Human development becomes
both the stabilizing force of society
and the engine of creation.

In the emergent era, learning environments become:
fields of resonance … not institutions of instruction

They are shaped to:
support emotional truth
activate intuition
foster deep reflection
deepen relational coherence
integrate conflict
expand creativity
allow emergence
connect learners to ideas that want to be created
cultivate embodied presence
support developmental safety
adapt fluidly to the learner
evolve with the community

They may appear as:

- learning ecosystems
- developmental communities
- embodied learning spaces
- creative collectives
- apprenticeships in living contexts
- cross-generational fields
- regenerative education networks

This is not schooling.

It is human evolution in practice.

In older systems:

- teachers instruct
- students absorb
- content is central
- authority is external

In resonant learning environments:

- guides steward emergence

A guide:

- listens deeply
- senses the field
- supports developmental edges
- holds emotional and relational safety
- evokes intuitive insight
- frames complexity
- models tri-level integration
- nurtures potential
- protects coherence

The guide's presence becomes the curriculum.

As learning becomes tri-level and emergent,
human potential evolves in recognizable ways:

- emotional resilience deepens
- relational intelligence matures
- intuition stabilizes
- creativity expands
- conflict integrates
- power aligns
- leadership becomes stewardship
- work becomes meaningful
- communities cohere
- institutions adapt
- society humanizes

Humanity becomes capable of living with complexity
without collapsing into fear or control.

When tri-level awareness stabilizes, performance stops fluctuating.
What is often called "peak performance" becomes the natural
operating state.

…

# THE LIVING PROTOTYPE

## Incubation in an Emergent World

Incubation in an emergent world is not what the current world calls an incubator:

not a startup program
not a mentor network
not an accelerator
not an entrepreneurship lab
not a consulting service
not a leadership training system
not an investment platform

A living prototype is something fundamentally different.

It is an ecosystem where the future described in this book becomes operational.

A living prototype is a place where:

tri-level awareness
resonance
emergence
coherence
human potential
idea-first creation
distributed intelligence
conflict-as-insight
relational growth
intuitive leadership
emergent power
developmental work
symbiotic innovation
resonant community

are not theories,
but lived conditions.
Such a prototype does not model the future.

It manifests it.

Every idea in this book carries a simple truth:

Humanity is entering a new phase of evolution,
but our structures are not built for that evolution.

Nowhere is this more visible than in entrepreneurship.

The startup ecosystem is built on:

- competition
- scarcity
- control
- extraction
- rational dominance
- emotional suppression
- investor pressure
- personal sacrifice
- high-risk / high-return gambling
- founder collapse
- short-term metrics
- unicorn mythology
- survival mentality

These assumptions actively suppress:

- intuition
- emergence
- human potential
- relational intelligence
- coherence
- developmental growth
- the true nature of ideas

The startup ecosystem is not broken.

It is built on a worldview
that no longer matches human development.

When a structure suppresses emergence,
it cannot be fixed through incremental improvement.

Something new has to be built …
not as an alternative system,
but as a **living reference**.

Living prototypes arise precisely at this threshold.

Most incubators begin with:

- curriculum
- program structure
- mentors
- workspace
- funding models

Living prototypes invert this logic.

They begin with …
the idea that wants to be created.

Ideas are not treated as proposals to be evaluated,
but as emergent intelligences to be listened to.

In such environments:

An idea signals itself.
A human senses it.
A field begins to form.
Human potential aligns to the idea.
Resources start to flow naturally.
Development unfolds.
Structure emerges.
An ecosystem takes shape.

The ecosystem organizes itself around the idea,
not the other way around.

This reversal is foundational.

Living prototypes tend to share a recognizable architecture.

**The Idea Holds the Wisdom**
Traditional systems analyze ideas.

Living prototypes listen to them.

Ideas are treated as:
- emergent intelligences
- carriers of their own rhythm
- holders of direction and timing
- organizers of people and resources

Ideas are not evaluated.

They are received.

**Human Potential Is the Core Resource**
In conventional models, people are assessed by:
- skills
- grit
- execution capacity

In living prototypes:
- inherent human resources are recognized
- subconscious patterns are gateways, not liabilities
- intuitive capacity is central
- personal development and idea development are inseparable
- relational coherence shapes outcomes

Humans are not trained to fit ideas.

Humans grow *with* ideas.

**Resonance Becomes the Operating System**

Decisions are guided by:

intuitive clarity
embodied sensing
relational attunement
field coherence
pattern recognition
emergent alignment

This is not pre-rational.

It is post-rational …
what becomes possible when rationality is integrated
into a larger field of awareness.

Resonance is not a preference.

It is the only mechanism capable of handling true emergence.

**Growth Is Developmental, Not Extractive**

In extractive systems, growth means:

acceleration
pressure
domination
compliance with external milestones

In living prototypes:

growth has rhythm
growth follows coherence
growth requires inner expansion
growth is symbiotic
growth aligns with the idea
growth unfolds at the pace of human development

This produces systems that are:
- emotionally grounded
- relationally coherent
- intuitively aligned
- structurally adaptive
- economically resilient

Growth becomes evolution,
not acceleration.

**Conflict Is Integration, Not Failure**
Conflict is inevitable where emergence is real.

In living prototypes, conflict is not feared.

It is used.

Conflict reveals:
- emerging truths
- misalignment
- subconscious patterns
- developmental edges
- unspoken needs
- evolving relational structure

By incubating the humans,
ideas can flow without distortion.

**The Ecosystem Becomes the Organism**
A living prototype is not a program.

It is:
- a relational field
- a living ecosystem
- an incubator of human potential
- a listening environment

a resonance amplifier
a coherence generator
a developmental container
an emergent structure
a prototype of a future societal unit

The ecosystem organizes itself around each idea
the way a womb organizes around a developing child.

This is not metaphorical.

It is structural.

Everything in the previous Chapters
has been pointing toward this threshold:
ideas that want to be created
tri-level awareness
emergent leadership
relational intelligence
power as alignment
conflict as insight
communities as coherent fields
institutions as living ecosystems
economics of resonance
learning as human evolution

A living prototype is where
these dynamics become operational.

It is the bridge
between conceptual architecture
and lived reality.

Not as a centralized answer …
but as a recognizable form
that can arise wherever conditions allow.

The living prototype is not the future.

It is a **signal**.

A signal that:

coherence can replace control
emergence can be held
ideas can be protected
human potential can lead
systems can evolve without force

What matters is not this prototype.

What matters is that
the pattern is now visible.

And once a pattern becomes visible,
it cannot be unseen.

…

## The Growth Lead

The traditional world has no equivalent for the Growth Lead.

Not founder.
Not coach.
Not investor.
Not facilitator.
Not mentor.
Not team lead.
Not strategist.
Not therapist.
Not advisor.

The Growth Lead is an emergent role
that appears only in ecosystems operating through
resonance, coherence, and tri-level awareness.

The Growth Lead is the person who:
senses the idea
protects its integrity
holds the coherence of the field
integrates conflict
sees subconscious patterns
stabilizes the ecosystem
aligns people with the idea
listens for what wants to be created
detects misalignment early
navigates emergence
supports developmental growth
amplifies intuitive clarity
creates the conditions for the idea to manifest

The Growth Lead is not leading the team.

They are leading the idea.

They are the guardian of emergence …
the relational membrane
between what exists
and what wants to be born.

In emergent creation, two realities are always present:

**The idea is ahead of humans.**
Ideas emerge from the opportunity field
and carry their own internal logic, coherence, and trajectory.

**Humans operate through layered awareness.**
Subconscious, emotional, rational, and intuitive layers
can become entangled, reactive, or misaligned.

This creates an inevitable tension:

The idea wants to move.
The humans are not yet ready.

Traditional systems respond to this tension by:
suppressing the idea
forcing the humans
abandoning the idea
pushing the team
compromising the idea's coherence

In ecosystems that honor emergence,
a different response becomes necessary …

A role appears that can hold
the evolutionary tension
without collapsing it.
That role is the Growth Lead.

The Growth Lead bridges:

the wisdom of the idea
the human system that must grow
the ecosystem that must stabilize

Without such a role,
ideas are distorted or lost.

With it,
ideas can unfold at their natural pace
while humans grow with them.

The Growth Lead is the only role in the ecosystem
whose responsibility is explicitly tri-level.

**Embodied Field**

They sense:

emotional truth
tension in the system
subconscious patterns
fear responses
survival dynamics
relational blockages
dissociation
somatic misalignment

They stabilize the nervous system of the ecosystem.

**Rational Field**

They bring:

clarity
precision
structure
insight

conceptual language
meaning-making
strategic framing
intellectual coherence

They articulate what the system is sensing
before the system knows how to say it.

**Intuitive Field**
They listen for:
the idea's direction
what wants to emerge
timing
pace
the next developmental step
subtle resonance shifts
energetic openings
intuitive clarity

They sense the future
before it becomes visible.

In older systems, leaders hold power.

In emergent ecosystems,
the Growth Lead holds:
coherence
resonance
direction
integrity
emergence

They do not:
control
command
demand

pressure
override
decide alone

The Growth Lead … leads
by stabilizing the environment
so the idea can lead.

Power does not sit in the role.

Power sits in the idea
and in the coherence of the field.

The Growth Lead ensures
that nothing interferes with that coherence.

In every emergent ecosystem,
the Growth Lead becomes the:
stabilizer
regulator
integrator
container for tension
translator of embodied patterns
normalizer of discomfort
space for emotional processing

This is why the Growth Lead must:
have a regulated nervous system
hold emotional charge
remain grounded in conflict
listen without collapsing
sense truth beyond words
avoid projection
stay unattached to outcomes
hold space without absorbing identity
remain connected to intuition under pressure

This is not a skill set.

It is a way of being.

**Protecting the Integrity of the Idea**
Ideas are fragile in their early stages …
not because they are weak,
but because humans have not yet grown enough
to hold their coherence.

The Growth Lead protects the idea from:
- fear
- urgency
- ego
- external pressure
- rational reduction
- emotional distortion
- premature scaling
- forced decisions
- misaligned structure
- subconscious sabotage
- relational misattunement

The idea does not need permission to exist.

It needs protection.

The Growth Lead is that protection.
**The Growth Lead and Conflict**
Conflict is inevitable wherever emergence is real.

The Growth Lead understands:
- conflict is not a problem
- conflict is insight
- conflict is information
- conflict is the next growth step

conflict reveals developmental edges
conflict exposes misalignment

The Growth Lead:
normalizes conflict
holds people safely through it
prevents collapse
prevents suppression
reveals deeper truth
integrates insight
realigns the system afterward

One of the Growth Lead's greatest gifts
is turning conflict into evolution.

**The Growth Lead and Founders**

Founders often carry:
deep intuitive resonance
strong embodied patterns
subconscious wounds
creative fire
loneliness
self-doubt
identity tension
emotional exhaustion

The Growth Lead sees the founder fully:
inherent resources
unintegrated patterns
intuitive brilliance
subconscious loops
fears and avoidances
undeveloped capacities
the developmental journey required

The Growth Lead does not fix the founder.

They support the founder
to grow with the idea.

This is not emotional dependency.

It is developmental partnership.

**The Growth Lead and the Team**

Within team dynamics,
the Growth Lead becomes:

the neutral center
the stabilizing field
the integrator of truth
the mirror of misalignment
the amplifier of resonance
the mediator of development
the guardian of coherence
the translator of the idea

The team does not align with the Growth Lead.

The team aligns with the idea,
through the field the Growth Lead holds.

**Why the Growth Lead Cannot Be the Founder**

This is one of the clearest truths in emergent creation …

The founder cannot hold the idea
and the field at the same time.

Because:

identity is tied to the idea
subconscious patterns activate
emotional entanglement arises
neutrality is lost
action replaces holding

team tension cannot be absorbed
fear distorts perception
the field destabilizes

Trying to be both
creates collapse.

The roles must be separated.

The idea needs a guardian.
The team needs a stabilizer.
Emergence requires neutrality.

The Growth Lead is not optional
where emergence is real.

But it is also not centralized, branded, or owned.

It is a role that:
appears when ideas outpace humans
stabilizes ecosystems under transformation
protects coherence during growth
enables emergence without force

The Growth Lead is:
the steward of emergence
the guardian of ideas
the holder of coherence
the translator of intuition
the integrator of conflict
the stabilizer of fields
the guide for human potential
the membrane between worlds

This role did not exist before
because the world did not yet require it.

It appears now
because emergence is accelerating
and humanity is learning how to grow with it.

…

## The Societal Membrane

Every evolutionary shift in human history requires a membrane.

A boundary between worlds.
A space where the old dissolves
and the new becomes possible.

Membranes perform three essential functions:

> **They protect what is emerging.**
>
> **They regulate what enters.**
>
> **They allow the new to take form without being crushed by the old.**

In biological systems, membranes allow cells to exist.
In ecosystems, membranes allow new species to form.
In consciousness, membranes allow new forms of awareness to stabilize.
In human development, membranes allow growth without overwhelm.

In periods of transition, a societal membrane becomes necessary.

Not as an institution,
but as a **function**.

**Why Society Needs a Membrane Right Now**
The world is in a liminal phase …

> Human potential is rising.
> Institutions are failing.
> Communities are fragmenting.
> Sensemaking is collapsing.
> The old logic is decaying.
> The new logic is emerging but not yet stable.
> Ideas are accelerating faster than human development.
> Technology is amplifying everything.

This creates global instability because:
the old system can no longer hold the complexity
the new system is not yet strong enough to stand on its own

Between these two worlds,
a membrane is needed.

A structure that:
protects new forms
stabilizes development
holds coherence
regulates pressure
nurtures emergent ideas
prevents premature collapse
supports human growth
aligns relational ecosystems
translates between old and new worlds
maintains integrity under tension

Wherever this function is present,
emergence becomes possible.

**What a Societal Membrane Actually Is**

A societal membrane is not:
a boundary that separates
a barrier that protects
a wall that isolates

A societal membrane is:
*a selective boundary*
*that allows the new to grow*
*while filtering out the distortions of the old.*

It is both:
permeable
protective

It is where:
emergence becomes form
potential becomes reality
possibility becomes structure
intuition becomes organization
resonance becomes ecosystem
coherence becomes institution

It is the zone of transition
where evolution becomes possible.

A societal membrane operates in two modes.

As a **passive** membrane, it:
blocks external distortions
filters out old-system pressures
protects ideas from premature rationalization
shields humans from destructive expectations
prevents fear-driven collapse
reduces noise
minimizes external chaos

It creates a space where:
intuition can speak
nervous systems can settle
relational patterns can be seen
conflict can be integrated
ideas can unfold coherently

This holding is quiet, without force or imposition.

As an **active** membrane, it:
stabilizes tension
mirrors misalignment
supports developmental growth
amplifies intuitive clarity

grounds the emerging ecosystem
translates emergence into form
integrates emotional dynamics
aligns human potential with ideas
stewards the rhythm of creation

The Growth Lead performs the fine-grained work
of this active membrane,
while the wider ecosystem
holds the structural boundary.

**Translation Between Worlds**

Every transitional era contains two operating languages.

The old system speaks in:
rational certainty
control
metrics
roles
performance
hierarchy
prediction
efficiency

The emergent system speaks in:
resonance
emergence
intuition
coherence
developmental rhythm
relational safety
distributed intelligence
holistic sensing

A societal membrane is bilingual.

It:

- translates emergence into rational clarity
- maps intuitive insight into tangible next steps
- expresses coherence in language old systems can hear
- explains ideas without compromising their essence
- bridges people, resources, and ideas
- protects the integrity of the new

while operating within the constraints of the old.

Without such translation,
emergence is either ignored or destroyed.

Ideas fail when pressure is wrong:

- too much → collapse
- too little → stagnation

The membrane regulates this pressure.

It:

- buffers external expectations
- slows premature acceleration
- limits destructive urgency
- prevents premature scaling
- protects the timing of emergence
- stabilizes emotional load
- contains relational triggers
- reduces internal chaos

This regulation is mostly invisible.

But it is the reason
emergence survives long enough
to become real.

**The Membrane as a Collective Nervous System**

A membrane is also the first form of a nervous system.
It senses:

what must enter
what must stay out
what must transform
what must slow down
what must accelerate
what is resonant
what is misaligned

In societal transition,
this sensing becomes distributed but coherent.

The membrane tracks:

the field
the idea
the humans involved
the ecosystem
timing
emotional truth
intuitive direction
relational dynamics
environmental pressure

This is not centralized intelligence.
It is **field intelligence**.

…

## Scaling Resonance in an Emergent World

Systems of the past scaled through:

- replication
- standardization
- institutionalization
- central control
- uniform programs
- hierarchical growth
- funding and infrastructure
- large-scale top-down design

These mechanisms cannot scale the emergent world.

They were built for:

- predictable environments
- stable markets
- industrial logic
- uniform human behavior
- compliance
- top-down authority

But the world now unfolding is:

- unpredictable
- emergent
- relational
- intuitive
- distributed
- developmental
- nonlinear
- in constant transformation

What is emerging cannot scale the old way.

It scales through resonance …
through human potential spreading like a field,
through ideas evolving across ecosystems,
through coherence reproducing itself.

What scales is not an incubator,
not a model,
not a program.

What scales is a **pattern**.

Traditional models scale by making copies:

copy the program
copy the curriculum
copy the structure
copy the brand
copy the process
copy the playbook
copy the rules

But resonance does not replicate.

It propagates.

Resonance spreads when:

people feel it
ecosystems sense it
ideas respond to it
founders recognize it
leaders orient toward it
communities align with it
institutions soften to it
systems reorganize around greater coherence

This is how coherence moves:
silently
subtly
steadily
through attunement
not through force

It is the only form of scaling
that does not collapse the integrity of what is emerging.

Resonance propagates across three interrelated levels.

**Individual Resonance**

*Personal transformation*

People who encounter this pattern often experience:
recognition of something long sensed but unnamed
release of suppressed emotional truth
deepening of intuitive access
reconfiguration of internal logic
a new relationship to power and conflict
a desire to live from coherence
a memory of who they are
a longing to step into their potential

This individual resonance spreads naturally
through relationships, decisions, leadership, and creative work.

This is the first level of scaling.
It is organic and unavoidable.

**Ecosystem Resonance**

*Relational and organizational transformation*

As individuals shift, ecosystems begin to evolve.

People start to:
integrate conflict instead of suppressing it
listen to intuition instead of overriding it
sense the field instead of forcing outcomes
create safety instead of pressure
amplify coherence instead of chaos
discover ideas instead of copying others
build relational ecosystems instead of hierarchies

Teams become more creative.
Organizations become more adaptive.
Communities become more aligned.
Ideas become more emergent.

Ecosystem resonance spreads
because it works.

**Societal Resonance**
*Structural transformation*

As coherence stabilizes across ecosystems:
new institutions begin to form
new economic patterns emerge
new leadership archetypes normalize
conflict is treated as relational insight
ideas outpace institutional suppression
human potential becomes a societal resource
people withdraw from structures that suppress growth
new forms of governance appear
new forms of collaboration arise

This is societal scaling.

It does not require revolution.
It requires **evolutionary coherence**.
Most incubators scale by:

- opening new offices
- hiring staff
- creating regional hubs
- franchising
- licensing programs

This pattern cannot scale that way
because replication destroys coherence.

You cannot copy:

- resonance
- intuition
- developmental timing
- relational safety
- emergent leadership
- tri-level integration
- conflict transformation
- idea-guided creation

These are not programs.

They are living patterns.

They propagate only
where conditions allow them to live.

This is biological scaling,
not industrial scaling.

What propagates is not an organization.

What propagates is an **operating logic**:

- ideas want to be created
- tri-level awareness enables creation
- human potential is the core resource
- resonance is the operating system

conflict is developmental information
coherence organizes systems
ecosystems behave like living organisms
emergence guides timing and direction
certain roles naturally appear
protective membranes stabilize growth
structure follows resonance
development precedes scale

This logic can manifest in many contexts:
incubation spaces
communities
startups
families
schools
institutions
governance experiments
organizations
networks
social movements
collaborative ecosystems

The pattern is not owned.

It is recognized.

As this pattern stabilizes,
certain functions begin to appear across society.

Growth Lead roles emerge in many contexts not as titles, but as developmental functions.

Resonant incubation spaces arise organically wherever ideas need protection and humans need growth.

Individuals begin to operate from integrated awareness, transforming leadership, relationships, and decision-making.

Ideas that want to be created find ecosystems capable of holding them.

Institutions begin reorganizing around human potential rather than control and extraction.

This is how a pattern becomes societal
without becoming centralized.

This pattern does not push itself outward.

People are drawn toward it
because they feel:

relief
recognition
resonance
possibility
coherence
alignment
clarity
freedom
truth
meaning

The moment of
*"Oh… this is what I've been sensing my whole life"*
is the mechanism of propagation.

Not marketing.
Not recruitment.
Not expansion.

Resonance.

There are places
where this coherence becomes particularly visible.

Such places function as:

reference points
stabilizing fields
calibration spaces
coherence attractors

…

# THRESHOLD

## When Growth No Longer Requires Collapse

For most of human history, growth has been inseparable from collapse.
Systems changed when they broke.
Old structures resisted until they failed.
Pressure accumulated until something gave way.

Through rupture, movement occurred.

This pattern shaped civilizations, institutions, and organizations. It also shaped how humans learned to relate to change itself.
Breakdown was not an exception; it was the mechanism.

When systems could no longer hold their own tension, collapse absorbed what could not be integrated.

Growth followed destruction.

Collapse did important work.
It discharged pressure that systems were unable to metabolize.
It resolved contradictions that could not be held simultaneously.
It reset dynamics that had become too rigid to adapt.

In this way, destruction functioned as a regulator.

Not because it was desired, but because nothing else could carry the load.

This pattern extended beyond institutions and societies. It shaped personal development, organizational change, and even how conflict was understood.

Transformation meant breaking something apart so something new could emerge.

What is becoming visible now is not the absence of tension, conflict, or instability.

It is something more subtle.

As awareness integrates … embodied, rational, and intuitive … growth no longer depends on collapse in the same way. Movement does not require failure to justify itself.

This does not mean pressure disappears.

The enemy dissolves.
But the pressure does not disappear.

What changes is **where that pressure goes**.

When collapse is no longer the default mechanism, pressure is no longer discharged through destruction.

Instead, it becomes available.
Available to be felt.
Available to be held.
Available to be sensed without immediate release.

This is not a moral achievement.
It is a structural shift.

What destruction once absorbed automatically now becomes visible to awareness.

For the first time, awareness can function as a **membrane** consciously.
Not as rulers.
Not as rebels.
But as a holding field.

A membrane does not stop pressure.
It does not eliminate difference.
It does not enforce harmony.

It allows tension to remain present without requiring immediate discharge.

This is not something a person *becomes*.
It is something that occurs when awareness is no longer outsourced to systems designed to collapse.

Whenever something genuinely new begins to emerge, resistance is inevitable.

Not because the system is failing,
but because coherence is being challenged.

What exists is not inert.
It is embodied, structured, and supported by rational understanding.
It makes sense … from within itself.

The new, by contrast, does not yet compute.

It is felt before it can be explained.
It carries potential before it carries proof.
It does not arise from what is wrong with the existing,
but from what wants to expand beyond it.

From within the existing system, this feels threatening.
From within the emerging movement, resistance feels obstructive.

Both perceptions are structurally real.

Resistance, in this sense, is not the enemy of emergence.
It is the **friction through which transition energy is generated**.

Resistance does not exist to make emergence harder.
It exists to give emergence form.

Without resistance, intuition remains unshaped … direction without substance.
It is through contact with what already exists … its constraints, its coherence, its embodied intelligence … that what wants to emerge becomes specific, grounded, and real.

Emergence is not formed in spite of resistance,
but through it.

The difficulty arises when this friction is interpreted through collapse logic.

Those connected to what is emerging often respond by
arguing for change …
trying to overcome resistance through explanation, persuasion,
or force.

In doing so, they enter what can be called the *resistance trap.*

> Resistance intensifies.
> Emergence pushes harder.
> Energy accumulates between the two.

Not because either is wrong,
but because both are responding from within the same logic that historically led to rupture.

In collapse-driven systems, this escalation eventually resolves through breakdown.

What becomes possible now is different.

When awareness can hold both coherences …
the legitimacy of what exists and the intention of what wants to emerge …
the friction does not need to discharge destructively.

Resistance is no longer something to defeat.
Emergence is no longer something to justify.

The energy between them becomes available
not for collapse,
but for reorganization.

In collapse-driven systems, power concentrates as tension rises.
Someone must decide.
Someone must enforce.
Someone must break the stalemate.

When awareness functions as a holding field, power no longer needs to dominate to move things forward.

It redistributes.
Not as equality.
Not as control.

But as coherence emerging where pressure is held rather than discharged.

This does not make systems gentle.
It makes them less destructive.

When collapse no longer absorbs pressure automatically, something changes in lived experience.

The pressure that once exited the system violently remains present longer.
The contradictions that once resolved through failure now coexist.

This is not a cost in the moral sense.

It is a consequence of pressure no longer being discharged through destruction.

Nothing is demanded.
Nothing is required.

What was once hidden becomes felt.

Human potential is not emerging to give us better solutions.

It is emerging to give us a different way of transitioning.
  Not faster.
  Not cleaner.

But less dependent on collapse as the engine of change.

This does not guarantee coherence.
It makes coherence possible without destruction.

…

## The Weight Before Reorganization

There is a reason this moment feels heavy.

Not overwhelming.
Not dramatic.
Heavy.

The weight does not come from crisis alone.
It comes from something more subtle.

What collapse once absorbed automatically
is no longer leaving the system in the same way.

In collapse-driven systems, pressure rarely lingered.
When tension grew too large, something broke.
Failure released what could not be integrated.
Destruction carried the excess.

This did not make collapse desirable.
But it made it functional.

Now, as collapse loses its central role,
that familiar discharge weakens.

Pressure does not vanish.
It stays.

This weight is not abstract.

It is felt as:
pause without clarity,
anger without a clear enemy,
tension without a release valve,
certainty dissolving without replacement.

This is not confusion.

It is the nervous system encountering pressure
that would previously have exited through rupture.

What was once discharged externally
is now encountered internally.

It is tempting to describe this as increased responsibility …
as though something new is being asked of us.

That framing is misleading.

What is changing is not what is required,
but what no longer absorbs pressure on our behalf.

Collapse once carried the excess automatically.
As that function weakens,
the same pressure becomes visible elsewhere.

Nothing is demanded.
Nothing is assigned.
Protection is simply no longer guaranteed.

This weight does not belong to a group,
a role,
or a type of person.

There are no designated holders of transition.

What is happening is conditional, not personal.

When collapse does not discharge tension,
holding occurs wherever awareness remains present.
  Not as effort.
  Not as virtue.
But as a consequence of staying.

This shift can feel isolating.

Not because others are absent,
but because familiar forms of shared release are gone.

Collapse once synchronized experience.
Everyone felt it when something failed.

Integration is quieter.

Pressure is encountered locally, somatically,
often without external validation.

This can resemble loneliness,
even when connection remains intact.

Another part of this weight is grief.

Not grief for what is lost,
but for what does not get to break.

Collapse offered finality.
Failure created endings.

Without collapse, endings stretch.
Contradictions coexist longer.
Resolution arrives slowly, if at all.

This grief is not pathological.

It is the body adjusting to continuity
where it once expected rupture.

Before another way of moving becomes available,
this transition is often lived as endurance.

Presence feels like holding.
Awareness feels like exposure.

Tension does not resolve.
Contradictions remain.
Meaning reorganizes slowly.

This is not alignment.

It is proximity.

Awareness is close enough to feel what is happening,
but not yet integrated enough to move with it.

Nothing noble is occurring.
Nothing is being proven.

What felt like "holding"
was not the future of human potential.

It was the absence of a familiar discharge.

This phase is not sustainable …
not because it is wrong,
but because it still relies on self-opposition.

Presence requires effort.
Awareness feels like endurance.
The system has not yet reorganized.

The weight was never the transition itself.

It was the last experience
before reorganization became possible.

When collapse no longer performs its old function,
pressure becomes available to awareness.

That is all.

Some will notice it immediately.
Others will not.

Both are normal.

This weight is not meant to be carried heroically.
It is not meant to be solved.

It is simply what becomes present
when growth no longer depends on collapse
to move forward.

And before another way of moving emerges,
this is how the threshold is felt.

…

## Allowing – When Friction Becomes Vitality

There is a quiet shift that happens when awareness settles into its full range.

The tension does not disappear.
The friction between what exists and what wants to emerge remains.
The pressure of transition is still present.

But something fundamental changes in how it is lived.

What once felt like hardship
no longer registers as opposition.

Under collapse-driven logic, friction is experienced as strain.

> Something to push through.
> Something to endure.
> Something to carry at personal cost.

The body tightens.
The mind braces.
The self separates from what is happening.

This is not weakness.
It is how humans learned to survive change when breakdown was the primary mechanism.

But when tri-level awareness becomes active, friction is encountered differently.

Not as resistance to overcome,
but as the medium through which form emerges.

The same tension is present …
yet it no longer pulls the individual away from themselves.

Allowing is often misunderstood.
It is not withdrawal.
It is not resignation.
It is not waiting.

Allowing is what happens when awareness is no longer fragmented.

When embodied response, rational understanding, and intuitive sensing are present at the same time,
the need to force resolution weakens.

The system does not stall.
It reorganizes.

Movement continues …
but without self-opposition.

One of the quiet miracles of this state is that individual and collective no longer compete.

There is no need to choose between personal alignment and systemic coherence.

As awareness holds multiple layers at once:
the individual responds truthfully,
the collective reorganizes organically.

No one takes on a role.
No one "holds" for others.

Coherence flows through those who are attuned … not because they are special, but because they are present.

This is not leadership.
It is resonance.

Human potential does not eliminate difficulty.

It eliminates the need to betray oneself in order to move forward.

The friction remains …
but it is no longer interpreted as punishment, cost, or burden.

It becomes the very experience of being alive at the edge of what is forming.

This is why those operating from human potential often describe the work as deeply meaningful, even when it is demanding.

Not because it is easy …
but because it is coherent.

The body recognizes alignment immediately.

Just as elite athletes do not seek comfort, but coherence,
humans operating from their full potential do not seek the absence of tension.

They seek the right tension.

> The kind that sharpens perception.
> The kind that deepens presence.
> The kind that allows something new to take form without tearing the self apart.

This is not transcendence.
It is embodiment.

There is nothing to adopt here.
Nothing to practice.
Nothing to become.

Allowing is not a method.

It is what naturally occurs
when awareness stops fighting its own signals.

What once felt like holding
is now simply being.

Embedded in what exists.
Open to what is emerging.
Moving with the system rather than against it.

This is the power the book has been pointing toward all along.
 Not control over the transition.
 Not acceleration of change.

But influence over how it is lived.

When enough individuals operate from this integrated state, pressure no longer needs to escalate into collapse to create movement.

Not because anyone intervenes …
but because the system has learned another way to reorganize.

…

## What Allows a Human to Remain Intact

Remaining intact is not a matter of endurance.

If it were, it would fail.

Endurance relies on holding tension still.
Integrity depends on circulation.

What allows a human to remain intact in periods of sustained pressure is not strength, discipline, or control,
but movement … continuous, multi-directional movement across layers of awareness.

Integrity is often mistaken for firmness.

In reality, it is fluid.

Pressure does not fracture a system because it is intense.
It fractures systems when pressure accumulates without movement.

Where circulation is present, pressure moves.
Where circulation stops, pressure concentrates.

Remaining intact is not about resisting force.
It is about allowing force to pass through without getting stuck.

In collapse-driven systems, excess pressure exited through failure.

Breakdown resolved what could not circulate.
Rupture released what awareness could not yet metabolize.

When that release mechanism weakens, pressure remains present longer.

This does not automatically create damage.

It creates a different requirement of organization.

Not something to do …
but something that must already be happening
for integrity to remain.

When integrity remains under sustained pressure, movement is occurring between layers of awareness.

Embodied signals register load before thought interprets it.
Rational understanding provides orientation without command.
Intuitive sensing adjusts timing rather than direction.

No layer dominates.
No layer is suppressed.

Circulation happens vertically, not hierarchically.

When this movement stalls …
when the body is overridden,
when the mind commands instead of listens,
when intuition is forced to justify itself …
pressure accumulates.

Integrity weakens not because awareness is insufficient,
but because circulation is interrupted.

The body is not a container for stress.

It is a sensor and regulator.

Signals such as fatigue, agitation, numbness, or urgency
are not signs of failure.

They indicate where circulation is slowing.

Remaining intact does not mean ignoring these signals.

It means responding before accumulation hardens into strain.

Listening downward is not introspection.
It is maintenance.

When pressure remains present, the mind often tries to compensate.
    It seeks certainty.
    It accelerates decision-making.
    It attempts to regain control.
This is understandable … and often counterproductive.

Integrity does not require the mind to disengage.
It requires the mind to relinquish command.

When rationality shifts from engine to compass,
it provides orientation without forcing resolution.

This allows movement to continue
even when outcomes are unclear.

Intuition does not push.

It signals when movement is possible
and when waiting preserves coherence.

Remaining intact depends on respecting timing
as much as direction.

Action taken too early fractures alignment.
Waiting too long concentrates pressure.

When intuition is allowed to inform timing without being overruled,
movement remains responsive rather than reactive.

Integrity is not maintained alone.

Circulation extends beyond the individual.

Relational contact … when present without projection or demand … provides external pathways for pressure to move.

This is not dependence.
It is hygiene.

Isolation concentrates load.
Resonant contact distributes it.

Remaining intact often coincides
with being seen without explanation.

Integrity is not balance.

Balance implies stability.
Integrity implies adaptability.

Dynamic coherence allows shape to change
without losing continuity.

This is why remaining intact often feels active rather than calm,
alive rather than resolved.

Nothing is frozen.
Nothing is suppressed.

Movement continues.

Remaining intact is not a personal capacity that some possess and others lack.

It is a condition that emerges
where circulation remains available
and pressure does not accumulate beyond movement.

It appears unevenly …
depending on context, timing, relational support, and load.

Nothing is being asked.
Nothing is being assigned.

Integrity either remains,
or it reorganizes until it does.

When humans remain intact under pressure,
systems do not need collapse to reset themselves.

Reorganization happens through movement,
not rupture.

This is not mastery.
It is function.

And it is already occurring
where conditions allow it.

…

## Where Power Actually Moves Now

Power has always been misunderstood.

Not because it is complex,
but because it changes form
whenever awareness changes.

What appears as power in one era
often becomes ineffective in the next …
not through failure,
but through misalignment.

In earlier systems, power concentrated vertically.

Decision-making, authority, and enforcement aligned around control.
This was not inherently corrupt.
It was coherent for the level of complexity those systems faced.

When information was scarce
and coordination costly,
centralized power reduced friction.

Hierarchy worked
because it matched the conditions of the time.

As complexity increases, structure becomes heavy.
  Decisions slow.
  Signals distort.
  Feedback arrives too late.
Power does not disappear in these moments.
It relocates.

Not upward.
Not downward.
Sideways … into the field.

In field-based systems, power is no longer something that can be held, claimed, or displayed.

It appears
where coherence is present.

It withdraws
where distortion accumulates.

This kind of power cannot be seized.
Attempts to grasp it collapse it back into older forms.

It is not wielded.
It is hosted.

Field power is not personal.

It does not belong to individuals, roles, or positions.
It arises situationally …
where signals are clear
and pressure circulates without concentration.

When coherence is present:
    noise drops,
    orientation sharpens,
    movement becomes possible without enforcement.

This is not influence through persuasion.
It is effectiveness through alignment.

Hierarchical systems rely on attribution.
    Who decided.
    Who approved.
    Who is responsible.

Field power disrupts this logic.

Impact occurs without clear authorship.
Direction emerges without command.
Change happens without visible authority.

This is not resistance to power.
It is power operating outside familiar forms.

When power operates as a field effect, distortion has consequences.

Not moral consequences.
Structural ones.

Where clarity is lost,
power thins.

Where signals are manipulated,
power fragments.

Where coherence is forced,
power collapses back into control.

No one is punished.
Nothing is judged.

The field simply stops responding.

This is the most difficult shift to accept.

Field power cannot be instrumentalized.

The moment it is used
to secure advantage,
assert dominance,
or control outcomes,
it withdraws.

Not in protest …
but because the conditions that allowed it
are no longer present.

One of the defining features of this shift
is that impact increasingly occurs
without recognition.

Changes take hold
without visible champions.
Movements gain momentum
without identifiable leaders.

This is not anonymity.
It is coherence expressing itself
where conditions allow.

In hierarchical systems, power protects itself.
　　It builds layers of insulation.
　　It controls access.
　　It resists feedback.
Field power does the opposite.

It remains exposed.

Not vulnerable …
responsive.

Exposure allows rapid correction,
fine-grained adjustment,
and continuous recalibration.

Armor would block the very signals
that make this power effective.

Power has not vanished.

It has not been taken.

It has moved
to where coherence can be held
without collapse.

This relocation does not announce itself.
It does not seek legitimacy.

It simply works …
until distortion returns.

…

## Standing When the World Polarizes

Polarization is not a moral failure.

It is a regulatory response.

When complexity exceeds a system's capacity to integrate,
the system simplifies.

It divides.

This division reduces internal tension by externalizing it.
What cannot be held together is pulled apart.

Polarization, in this sense, is not regression.
It is an attempt at stabilization.

As polarization intensifies, meaning itself becomes dangerous.
Nuance is experienced as betrayal.
Uncertainty is interpreted as weakness.
Questions feel like attacks.

Rationality does not disappear.
It weaponizes.
Arguments sharpen.
Positions harden.
Language narrows.

At the same time, intuitive sensing is suppressed.
The future collapses into threat.
Only the present battle remains legible.

This is not ideological failure.
It is nervous-system overload
expressed at scale.
In polarized systems, explanation does not resolve tension.

It amplifies it.

Each argument introduces new information
that must be evaluated under threat.

The system responds by further simplification.
Sides become clearer.
Lines are drawn more sharply.

This is why persuasion rarely works
when polarization is active.

The system is not seeking understanding.
It is seeking relief.

What interrupts polarization is not opposition
and not agreement.

It is standing.

Not as a personal stance,
but as a field effect.

Standing occurs
when pressure is present
and not immediately discharged
into reaction.

It is the moment where escalation pauses
because nothing is fed into it.
    No argument is added.
    No side is taken.
    No counterforce is applied.
The circuit loses energy.

Standing is often mistaken for neutrality.

It is not.

Neutrality withdraws engagement.
Standing remains present.

Standing does not avoid tension.
It allows tension to be felt
without converting it into opposition.

This is regulation, not withdrawal.

When standing occurs, it often looks quiet.

A pause instead of a response.
A question instead of a claim.
Silence instead of escalation.

These are not tactics.

They are natural consequences
of pressure being held
without reaction.

Standing cannot be performed.
It cannot be maintained through effort.

It emerges
when awareness remains integrated
under load.

One of the reasons standing feels uncomfortable
is that it lacks attribution.

> There is no visible action.
> No identifiable intervention.
> No immediate outcome.

From within polarized systems,
this can look like absence.

In reality, it is stabilization.

Pressure that is not converted into reaction
begins to redistribute.

The field reorganizes
without force.

Polarization creates urgency.

Everything feels immediate.
Delays feel dangerous.

Standing introduces timing.

Not waiting as avoidance,
but waiting as synchronization.

Action taken from urgency
feeds polarization.

Action taken from timing
reduces it.

This distinction cannot be explained into existence.
It is sensed.

Standing does not always occur.

Sometimes pressure exceeds integration capacity.
Sometimes reaction happens.

This is not failure.

It is information.

The system is showing
where circulation is not yet available.

Standing is not a permanent state.
It appears and disappears
as conditions allow.

When standing occurs in multiple places,
polarization loses momentum.

Not because agreement is reached,
but because escalation is no longer fueled.

The system does not collapse.
It does not resolve.

It recalibrates.

This is not transformation through victory.

It is stabilization through non-escalation.

…

# THE EMERGENT FUTURE

## The World That Emerges

The world that emerges is not imagined.
It is already forming.

Not as a blueprint.
Not as a system.
Not as a plan.

But as a shift in how life organizes itself
when human potential is no longer suppressed
and emergence is allowed to unfold.

This world does not arrive all at once.
It appears gradually, unevenly, quietly …
through people, communities, institutions, and cultures
that begin to operate from resonance rather than control.

What follows is not a vision of the future.
It is a description of what becomes visible
when the impasse has been crossed
and coherence begins to replace fragmentation.

In this emergent world, decisions are no longer driven primarily by:

fear
urgency
control
prediction
authority
optimization
domination

They are guided by:

- resonance
- coherence
- intuition
- relational truth
- developmental timing
- collective sensing
- emergent clarity

This does not make the world vague or unstructured.
It makes it *alive.*

Direction is no longer imposed.
It is sensed.

Action is no longer forced.
It unfolds.

In this world, human potential is no longer treated as:

- a resource to be extracted
- a variable to be optimized
- a risk to be managed
- a cost to be reduced

It becomes the primary organizing principle
of work, learning, leadership, economy, and society.

People are valued not for what they produce,
but for their capacity to:

- sense
- relate
- grow
- integrate conflict

navigate uncertainty
hold complexity
create meaning
align with what wants to emerge

This shift changes everything …
quietly, structurally, irreversibly.

Institutions in the emergent world no longer exist
to stabilize the past.

They exist to support life as it evolves.

They become:
adaptive rather than rigid
relational rather than bureaucratic
coherent rather than hierarchical
developmental rather than extractive
intuitive as well as rational

Their legitimacy no longer comes from authority.
It comes from resonance.

They are trusted
because they listen.

Work in this world is no longer organized
around survival, sacrifice, or exhaustion.

It becomes a primary arena
for human development.

Work:
strengthens awareness
deepens relational capacity
sharpens intuition

integrates emotion
reveals subconscious patterns
aligns people with ideas
creates meaning through contribution

Productivity becomes a side effect.
Value emerges naturally
when humans are allowed to grow.

The economy of the emergent world
is no longer built on scarcity and extraction.

It reflects:
creativity
regeneration
contribution
coherence
alignment
potential

Value is recognized where life expands …
not where it is depleted.

Capital flows toward coherence.
Resources follow resonance.
Wealth is measured in flourishing.

**Education as Evolution**

Learning is no longer preparation for life.

It *is* life.

Education becomes:
continuous
embodied

relational
intuitive
developmental
emergent

Humans learn by:
participating
sensing
reflecting
creating
integrating
evolving

Knowledge no longer dominates.
Awareness does.

In the emergent world, conflict is not avoided or weaponized.

It is listened to.

Conflict reveals:
misalignment
suppressed truth
developmental edges
relational tension
emerging direction

When held in coherence,
conflict becomes one of the system's
most reliable sources of intelligence.

This world has no capital.
No headquarters.
No movement.
No leader.

No founder.
No institution at its center.

It is distributed,
emergent,
relational.

It appears wherever:
humans choose coherence over control
resonance over force
development over domination
truth over performance

It spreads not by expansion,
but by recognition.

This world is not coming.

It is already here …
in fragments,
in moments,
in relationships,
in decisions,
in quiet acts of courage,
in choices to listen rather than react,
in systems that soften rather than harden.

What is new
is not the world itself,
but the capacity to recognize it.

Nothing in this world needs to be built from scratch.

What is required is:
the courage to stop suppressing what is alive
the patience to let coherence organize itself
the willingness to grow with what emerges

The future does not need to be created.

It needs to be allowed.

…

## The Invitation

*For Those Who Feel the Resonance*

This book is not written for everyone.

It is written for those who feel something …
even if they cannot name it yet.

A quiet knowing.
A subtle pressure.
A sense that the world they see
is not the world they fully belong to.

A recognition that something deeper is possible,
not through struggle or force,
but through coherence, resonance,
and the untapped potential already inside them.

If you have felt this …
even once …
this chapter will feel familiar.

Not because it is calling you,
but because it is describing something
you already know.

This book tends to resonate with those who:

- feel the intuitive pull of ideas they cannot yet explain
- sense meaning in places others overlook
- live with the tension between who they are and who they are becoming
- perceive dynamics beneath the surface of conversations
- experience conflict as a doorway, not a threat
- feel when something is off before knowing why
- have lived with the frustration of being "ahead of their time"
- often feel alone in how deeply they see

feel constrained by the limits of current structures
long for a world where they can be fully themselves
carry ideas that seem too large for traditional systems
sense potential in people they cannot yet see
resonate with a future they cannot fully describe

If any of these feel true,
it is not accidental.

What is already happening in you
is being named here.

Humanity is in the midst of a transition:
from suppression to coherence
from control to resonance
from fragmentation to integration
from rational dominance to tri-level awareness
from extraction to human potential
from authority to emergent leadership
from linearity to emergence
from institutions to ecosystems
from ideas as property to ideas as wisdom
from fear-driven conflict to developmental conflict
from hierarchical organization to living fields

This transition is not theoretical.

It is already alive
in people who feel:
the friction
the mismatch
the longing
the potential
the ache
the future
the truth

This ache is not a problem.

It is an activation.

It means something in you
is already responding to the new world
before it has language.

**You Are Not Alone**

One of the most difficult experiences
for those who sense what is emerging
is the feeling of being alone.

> Alone in vision.
> Alone in sensitivity.
> Alone in depth.
> Alone in emotional truth.
> Alone in the capacity to hold tension.
> Alone in the coherence longed for.
> Alone in intuitive knowing that has no obvious place.

This loneliness is not a flaw.

It is a signal.

It means you are among the first
to feel the shift.

What you sense is real.
What you feel is valid.
What you know matters.

And there are others.

You are not alone in this resonance.

You are part of a field …
one that is growing, aligning,
and remembering itself.

This was never invented.
It is simply being recognized.

This is not an invitation to:
- join something
- follow a system
- adopt a method
- take a program
- become part of a movement

Those are forms the old world relies on.

What is happening here is quieter.

It is a remembering of:
- who you are
- what you sense
- what you have always known
- the potential you have held back
- the truth you tried to fit into smaller shapes
- the coherence you have longed for
- the ideas that have stayed with you
- the subtle intelligence within you
- the resonance that feels like home

This book does not offer you a place.

It reflects the place
you have already been standing.

What tends to unfold next is not forceful.

People who recognize themselves here
often find that:

growth becomes the foundation of their work
intuition regains legitimacy
embodied truth is no longer suppressed
tension becomes developmental rather than threatening
ideas reveal themselves more clearly
relationships reorganize around coherence
work aligns with who they are becoming

Nothing needs to be forced.

Alignment precedes movement.
Coherence shapes direction.

Not everyone will read this book.
Not everyone will understand it.
Not everyone will feel it.

And that is not a problem.

Because the future does not emerge
through comprehension alone.
It emerges through sensing.

Those who can feel coherence,
    who notice resonance,
    who sense potential in others,
    who carry tension without collapsing,
    who listen beneath the surface …

are already participating
in what is unfolding.

If you can feel this book,
nothing new is being asked of you.

You are already inside the movement of it.

…

## Closing: The Field That Holds Us

There is a moment in every creation
when the language becomes quiet
because the field itself is speaking.

This is that moment.

This book has not been a description of a new system.
It has been a remembering.

A remembering of how we create,
  how we sense,
  how we grow,
  how we relate,
  how we listen,
  how we become human
in a world that is changing.

It has been a remembering
of what lives underneath everything:
  the embodied truth we carry
  the rational clarity we seek
  the intuitive intelligence that guides us
  the ideas that call us
  the relationships that shape us
  the ecosystems that hold us
  the potential that longs to move

This was never invented.
It simply became visible.

The world you have been sensing your whole life
is already here.

This book has helped name
what was already present.

The field that holds us:
is older than our institutions
is wiser than our beliefs
is deeper than our identities
is subtler than our strategies
is closer than our thoughts
is quieter than our fears

We have always been connected to it,
even when we forgot.

What has changed is not the field.

What has changed
is our awareness of it.

This book has been a process
of turning toward the field
instead of away from it.

A process of:
remembering what we already know
trusting what we already feel
sensing what we already hear
allowing what we already are

This is not an ending.

It is a pause
inside a much longer movement.

At certain moments,
in certain places,
this field takes form.

Not as ownership.
Not as authority.
Not as a center.

But as gestures.
As expressions.
As living demonstrations
that coherence is possible.

These expressions appear,
do their work,
and dissolve back into the field.

What matters is not their name.

What matters is that
the pattern is now recognizable.

And once a pattern is recognizable,
it no longer belongs to anyone.

The work of the future
does not belong to an organization,
a system,
or a framework.

It moves through people
who can feel resonance.

People who:

- sense alignment
- feel tension as developmental pressure
- understand conflict as truth
- recognize ideas as living forces
- desire coherence
- listen intuitively

grow through emergence
anchor themselves in embodied clarity
create from honesty
build through relationship
lead through presence

These people carry the pattern
into places no book can reach.

Into families.
Into relationships.
Into organizations.
Into communities.
Into institutions.
Into everyday life …

where change actually begins.

This is how a new world emerges …
through people who feel the field
and live from it.

If this book has offered anything,
let it be these recognitions:

**You are not alone in what you sense.**
There are others who feel the same shift.

**Your potential is not an individual challenge.**
It is a shared human capacity.

**Your intuition is not irrational.**
It is a form of intelligence
the world is learning to hear again.

**Your emotional truth is not a weakness.**
It is a stabilizing force.

**Your ideas are not accidents.**
They are signals of what wants to be created.

**Your way of seeing is not strange.**
It is timely.

**Your longing is not a flaw.**
It is orientation.

These are not instructions.

They are reminders.

## A Quiet Closing

There is no call to action.
No path to follow.
No identity to adopt.

The field will continue to speak.
Your intuition will continue to respond.
Your potential will continue to unfold.

You will know what to do
not because you are told,
but because you can feel it.

Nothing needs to be joined.
Nothing needs to be proven.

What matters
is already moving through you.

## End of the Book … Beginning of the Field

We close these pages,
but not the field.

The field remains.

Open.
Alive.
Unfinished.

Wherever you go from here,
go with the knowing
that you are already part
of something quietly profound.

The world that wants to emerge
is already holding you.

And you are already holding it.

www.ingramcontent.com/pod-product-compliance
Lightning Source LLC
LaVergne TN
LVHW010642110826
845149LV00014B/2931

* 9 7 9 8 9 9 4 9 8 9 9 0 6 *